SUCCESSFUL SELLING

HOW TO ATTRACT, MANAGE, CLOSE AND KEEP MORE BUSINESS IN A BUYER-CENTRIC WORLD

by Matt Heinz

WANT MORE IDEAS AND INSPIRATION?
Check out Matt's blog at:
http://www.MattonMarketingBlog.com

Copyright © 2010 by Heinz Marketing
All rights reserved.

ISBN: 978-0-615-36409-4

Art Direction and Design:
TinyTee Graphics • Teena Brugh
www.tinyteegraphics.com

Published by Heinz Marketing Press
9394 NE 120th Place
Kirkland, WA 98034

Printed in the United States of America

~~~~~~~~~~~~~~~~~~~~~~~~~~~~~~~~~~~~~~~

This book is dedicated to my wife, Beth.

She knows why.

~~~~~~~~~~~~~~~~~~~~~~~~~~~~~~~~~~~~~~~

TABLE OF CONTENTS

TABLE OF CONTENTS

TABLE OF CONTENTS

~~~~~~~~~~~~~~~~~~~~~~~~~~~~~~~~~~~~~~

Introduction

~~~~~~~~~~~~~~~~~~~~~~~~~~~~~~~~~~~~~~

Many of the best sales strategy books I've read have been far too long.

They make great points, prove them with case study after case study, and both individually and collectively represent some of the best sales insight I've gathered. They just take too long to read.

If you're like me, you're pulled in 20 directions every day. Harried at work, stuck in traffic, the emails never stop, and family's waiting at home. As much as I'd love to have time to read more of the sales, marketing and business books stacking up in my office, there aren't enough hours in the day, or days in the year.

Which brings me to this book. Yes, it's a book – but it's really a compilation of more than 60 "books". The idea was to provide a loosely organized set of ideas, insights and best practices that get you thinking about your sales strategy (as well as the underlying tactics) in a fresh way. You can read the book front to back, or just flip through and find something of interest today. Get in, get out.

But when you're done with a particular chapter or article, take a few moments to make the connection back to your business. These topics are meant to introduce an idea, knead it a bit to help you understand the context, intent and objective, then give you the space to personalize the implications for your business, your job or your career.

For example, after reading each piece, ask yourself these questions:

- How does this apply to my business? How could this make a difference in my objectives and desired outcomes?
- What specifically could I do differently because of this?
- What's the next step to explore or implement this?
- How will I measure its success?

With that, let's get after it. Thanks for reading, and please let me know not just what you learn, but what you've done with it.

**Matt
Heinz**
matt@heinzmarketing.com

~~~~~~

Preparation & Productivity

~~~~~~

How to Get Three Hours Back Every Day - Eliminate Distractions & Use Your Down Time

I need more hours in the day, and I assume you do as well. Between our personal and professional lives, there's always too much to do and not enough time to do it.

But despite these challenges, I'm constantly looking for ways to do two things:

1. Eliminate distractions
2. Make better use of "down time"

If you're trying to do the same, here are eight things I'd recommend trying. Collectively, I think they effectively give me back about three hours every day.

Don't drive

We waste a lot of time in the car, driving. Except for returning a few phone calls, this isn't very productive time typically. If you can take the bus, other public transportation or even carpool with coworkers, you can use part of that time to get caught up on other work. Catch up on email offline, brainstorm something without other distractions and work through other things on your to-do list. Worst case; catch up on some of your reading. Any of that is better than stop-and-go traffic.

Always have something to read with you

Everywhere you go, carry something you want to read. It can be printed materials (newspapers, magazines, printed-out articles) or it can be saved content on your smartphone. For example, on my iPhone I have access to my RSS feeds via Google Reader, a mobile version of ReadItLater that syncs Web articles I want to read, and also an iPhone version of Kindle software to catch up on a book I'm reading. There are so many times during the day when I'm waiting, or in a line, that can be used for a few minutes to catch up on some of this.

Avoid and cancel meetings

Do you really need to attend every meeting on your schedule? Have you yourself scheduled meetings that can be more effectively handled with a 5-10 minute conversation in the hallway? I'd be willing to bet that 25% of your meetings this week aren't worth your time. Figure out which ones they are, and get your time back.

Keep your email offline, all the time

If you use Outlook in particular, right-click on the icon in the lower right-hand corner of your screen and select "Work Offline." This will essentially "freeze" the email in your inbox currently, and queue up anything in your Outbox to sync when you want to. This helps you focus on what's at hand, without getting distracted in real-time by new incoming messages. Click the send/receive button when you want to, but otherwise stay more focused and more productive without the constant distractions.

Forward your phone to voicemail when you need/want to focus

Most phones and phone systems give you the ability to point inbound calls directly to voicemail. If you need to focus on something, shouldn't you turn off this distraction as well? You don't have to do this all day. But if the project in front of you will take 30 minutes to get done, don't let things like new emails and phone calls distract you. That 30-minute project could take 60-90 minutes easy if you check email, take a call and have to get re-engaged and focused again.

Get up earlier

Would it really be that hard to get up 30 minutes earlier? This may not be your most productive awake time. But an extra 30 minutes (when the rest of the house is still sleeping) could be used for reading, exercise, whatever you want. This alone gives you an extra 3.5 hours a week, and that's a lot of time.

Do your most important 1-2 tasks/projects FIRST every day   (before email and voicemail)

At the beginning of each day, you already know what 1-2 things are most important to accomplish. But most of us, before tackling those projects, check email and voicemail and quickly get distracted by the day's interruptions and fire-drills. Nine times out of ten, those distractions can wait until your most important tasks are finished. Get them done first, and I guarantee you'll feel (and be!) far more productive every day.

Delegate

You probably aren't delegating to others actively enough. You're probably doing too much yourself, including things that might be more efficient to be done by others (and sometimes with better results). You could be using a service like TimeSvr to get small tasks done by someone else. You could use eLance to outsource a variety of administrative projects. You could use ActiveWords to shortcut frequently-used activities on your computer. Long story short, you're working too hard and doing too much. Do less yourself, but get the same and more done.

 ## Use the Five Minute Rule to Get Intimidating Projects Done

We all have big, intimidating projects on our plates that, frankly, are a little scary. They either feel like a lot of work, or you're not exactly sure how to tackle them. So, we hem and haw and avoid them.

I've found that a fairly simple trick can help me get more of those projects done. It takes just five minutes.

When I'm facing a big project or task, I tell myself I'm going to spend five minutes getting it started, and that's it. I'm either going to just do five minutes worth of that task, or just spend five minutes planning how to tackle it.

The secret of the Five Minute Rule is that I almost always keep going, blow past the five minutes, and get the task done in far less time than if I would have kept procrastinating.

It's those five minutes that demonstrate how relatively quickly and easily the task can actually get done. If you get five minutes of momentum, sometimes that's all you need to keep going to the finish. If you use the five minutes to brainstorm, it makes the task far less intimidating and easier to get done right away.

Find something on your list right now and give it five minutes. Let me know what happens next.

☑ Five Ways to Stay Focused, Get More Done & Be More Successful

I recently asked several business and executive coaches what they do for their clients. I wanted to know more about their process, their approach and generally how they create value for the people and organizations they engage.

Although each had a slightly different take, it all boiled down to one thing – focus. Each successful coach produced results for their clients by helping them get the most out of themselves and their teams, in every case by focusing time, talents, resources and values.

What I heard generally fell into five distinct areas of focus:

1. **Focus on what's important.** It's easy to feel successful in a day that's busy. Filled with putting out fires. Getting things done. But often, we don't get the right things done. By stepping back and focusing on what's most important (not necessarily what's in front of us, or what's easiest, or what's screaming the loudest), we make far better forward progress (and often in less time).

2. **Focus on what you're good at.** Know your strengths, and lean into them. Compare that to what your organization needs, and ensure that others are doing everything else for you. Yes, there's a cost to delegating, but the results will far outweigh the investment when you have more time for your strengths, and others are accelerating your cause by leveraging theirs.

3. **Focus on fewer things.** Most of us take on far too much. Even if those are all things that are both important and speak to our strengths, there's not enough time in the day to get it all done. Make the hard trade-offs for what's going to drive the most value, and make the hard decisions to put other projects on the back-burner.

4. **Focus on the basics.** What's most important to your business? What's fundamental? What got you where you are now? What are your values? Getting back to the basics of your business can oftentimes be the simplest and most effective way to accelerate growth and productivity again.

5. **Focus on what you want.** It's amazing to me how many people let the day and its myriad influences direct not just day-to-day, but larger directional decisions that affect personal and professional success. When's the last time you took 30 minutes to reflect on what's most important to you? What will make you happiest and fulfilled? How do you map those priorities back to your life and your business?

Of course, achieving one or many of these areas of focus is far easier said than done. If you have the discipline to address and stick to these on your own, you're in the minority. For the rest of us, finding a coach (or even just a mentor) to keep us accountable and help unlock the full potential of our focus can reap significant dividends personally and professionally.

 ## Seven Proven Tips for Conquering the Email Mountain

While working through a particularly gnarly problem with our company's virtual helpdesk, I was told that my email usage (measured largely by the size of my deleted items folders) is in the top 5% of users they see across their various clients.

This actually surprised me, in that I had always assumed that others get much more email volume than I typically do. This assumption is based on frequent observation of colleagues and friends with overloaded inboxes, sometimes with hundreds of unread emails. These colleagues talk about drowning in their email, which makes both focus and staying on top of things far more difficult.

Despite my high inbound email volume, my inbox is almost always empty. What's more, I have peace of mind in knowing where (and how) to find anything, and have built myself an email system that allows me to tackle every email "action" in the right time.

The net result of this system is that I no longer let my email run my day. I can stay focused on what's most important throughout the day, get to my email when I *need* to, and still keep the inbox clean.

How? Listed below are my top seven best practices:

(Note: These tips assume you're using Microsoft Outlook as your email client, although some will work with Gmail and other Web email services as well).

1. **Rules:** I aggressively use Outlook's email rules to manage my inbox. This automates much of the filing and sorting I'd otherwise have to do manually, especially when Outlook can recognize patterns and help me save certain types of emails for quick scanning or processing later. For example, I subscribe to several email newsletters, but every one is automatically filed in a "reading" folder (more on that below). I get "watched item" alerts from eBay, which also get filed in a separate folder. There are certain reports I'm copied on, which I found that I rarely read but want filed away for future reference. I have an Outlook rule that does this filing for me automatically. This tool alone saves me countless clicks and minutes every day.

2. **Three main folders:** For short-term processing, I typically sort the rest of my email into three folders: Action, Waiting For and Reading.

    *   *Action*: If I receive an email that can be responded to in two minutes or less, I just tackle it right away. Any degree of procrastination on such a short-term task can literally double (or worse) the amount of time I spend on it. Anything else that takes longer than two minutes goes into the Action folder. Very, very few of these requests need *immediate* response. Putting them together in an "action" folder allows me to tackle them later, and all at once.

    *   *Waiting for*: I often send an email to a colleague or vendor, and wait for a response. I typically blind-copy myself on these emails, and have an Outlook rule set up so that these emails automatically get sorted into a "Waiting For" folder. This gives me a complete inventory of the outstanding emails I've sent for which I haven't received a response. I'll quickly scan this folder a few times a week, deleting emails that have been responded to, and occasionally following up with people that haven't yet taken action.

    *   *Reading*: I get to this once a day, usually on the bus in the morning or evening. None of it is urgent, and I have no problem deleting an unread newsletter if the folder is getting too large, or if more recent emails (especially in the case of news summaries) are piling up.

    I file these folders in my Outlook folders with an "@" symbol in front of them, so that they all stack up at the *top* of my Outlook folders list. This way they're always in front of me for easy clicking and viewing when I'm ready.

3. **Work in offline mode:** This is a great way to stay focused on what you're currently doing, and not get distracted by new emails coming in. Plenty of productivity experts tell their clients to turn off "new email" notifications already - get rid of the little beep, the preview pane, the "new email" graphic in the taskbar. All of those suggestions are moot if you work offline. How often you click that send/receive button is up to you. Many gurus suggest you don't need to check your email more than 1-2 times a day. I'm more addicted to email than that, but still typically go at least 30-60 minutes between checks. This helps me stay focused on getting the right things done in the meantime.

4. **Keep storage folders for *everything*:** I keep folders in Outlook for everything, and open new folders on a regular basis. I try to organize them in a consistent manner, and use lots of subfolders. This gets anything that no longer needs an action - that's purely for future reference - out of sight but within reach.

5. **Xobni:** This Outlook add-on has saved me hours of searching through email archives, and I've only had it for about a month. In a nutshell, Xobni is a search engine for your email, and sits on the right-hand side of your screen. It allows you to search names and keywords, pulling up associated contacts, consolidating document attachments and more. I've found it invaluable, especially if you aggressively store archived emails in folders like I do, and don't always remember where you put everything.

6. **Use Outlook's PST archive folders 2-4 times a year:** If you get a lot of email, and store much of it for future reference, your folders will get really big, really fast. Use Outlook's PST archive folders to create "offline" storage tanks for long-past emails. This will clear up space (and improve performance) with your account on the Exchange Server, but keeps those old emails within reach. You can even set up rules in Outlook to automatically archive files into your PST folders after a certain # of days.

7. **Unsubscribe!** We all end up on too many distribution and subscriber lists. If you're unsure if you want to stay on those lists or not, simply set up an Outlook rule. But if you find you never read them, unsubscribe. It'll be that many fewer emails in your inbox and you can always re-subscribe if you really need it or miss it.

Time for Reflection

In a story about Turner Broadcasting and CEO Phil Kent in *Business Week,* Kent shared his three-part "CEO Manual":

1. Carve out time to think, not just react
2. Sabbaticals give you useful perspective
3. Don't over schedule; leave time for colleagues

In smart organizations that focus on execution and results, time for reflection is still vital. Do that on a regular basis, and the "snap" decisions we're all required to make on a daily basis will be far more informed and rooted in what's most important.

Dealing with Information Overload

Every day, we're faced with far more information to consume than we can possibly manage. Ignoring the stuff we don't care about is easy, but even the emails, blogs, magazines, newsletters and other information we *do* care about can pile up far faster than we can consume it.

This is an every day problem that's made worse after an extended period away from the office. I recently took a week off with my family - no email, no cell phone, no connection to the real world - and came back to an avalanche of information. More than 1,000 emails to digest, more than 1,300 unread blog posts in my RSS feed, a large stack of magazines and mail, etc.

But we all know that the problem of information overload isn't confined to the day after a vacation. None of us can get through even the pre-filtered information that comes at us each day, and it's quite stressful to think we're "missing out" on something important buried in that stack.

The strategy I'm using this morning is really no different than what I do every day to manage that stack of incoming information. My simple strategy is as follows:

Sort
Know what information is required, and what's optional. The stack of information you *must* consume is likely quite small, and very manageable on a regular basis.

Skip
Don't worry about reading everything. If you're reading just *some* of the information in front of you, you're already doing far better than the vast majority of your colleagues and peers.

Skim
Read quickly. Skim headlines, flip pages of magazines quickly and look only for content that piques your interest. Focus on just the first couple paragraphs of any piece that interests you. Continue reading if you're truly interested, otherwise move on quickly to the next piece. Chances are those first couple paragraphs gave you the gist of what you needed to know anyway.

Save
Don't worry about reading everything right away. If you find something you want to read but don't have time right away (a longer article, a White Paper, etc.), file it in a "reading" folder. I have one in my email inbox, as well as a physical "reading" folder that stays with me at office and home, so I can easily pick something out when the time is right.

 ## Being Busy
vs. Being Focused

We're all busy. But that's not the issue.

The issue is whether or not you can comfortably accommodate new work without getting frustrated, flustered or immobilized. That's the test.

If you feel completely overwhelmed by something new on your plate, frustrated when your boss asks for something new or flustered when the list of projects in your lap continues to grow, you're clearly not alone. That happens to all of us. But if you don't have an effective system (no matter how simple or complex) to rationalize those new ideas against what's currently on your plate, then you might just be unfocused.

If you don't know how to evaluate new ideas against those you're already focused on, work with your manager (or have a quick meeting-of-one) to make sure you both agree on what's most important in your role, your department and your company. Clarity over underlying values and objectives will be your compass by which to evaluate and triage every new idea.

Your plate's only so big, and your time is incredibly valuable. You owe it to yourself to work only on the things that are going to deliver the most value to your organization, and the most satisfaction and productivity for yourself.

Busy is good. Too busy is bad. And I guarantee that something on your plate, right now, shouldn't be there.

Can you find it?

All of it?

Outsource Your Reading

Want to read more, but just don't have the time? Let someone else read for you!

It's not crazy. There are a number of tools, most online and many for free, where basically someone else does the "heavy lifting" of reading *everything*, summarizing what's most important and prescient for you.

In just a few minutes, you can read five daily newspapers.

In just four pages, you can read and entire business book.

In a single screen, you can consume a week's worth of a dozen blogs.

Don't believe me?

The *Wall Street Journal's* Morning Brief email: Available for subscribers only, this morning email (every day except Sunday) gives a real-time, morning-of summary of what's become news since the print edition went to press the night before. Even more interesting is the bottom-half of the email, which summaries (and links to) news stories from a wide, wide variety of other publications. It's a great way to catch up on interesting news from corners of the publishing world I rarely get to personally, and it takes less than a minute to scan each day.

ExecuBooks: For just over a dollar a week, this service offers an archive of hundreds of popular business books covering a wide range of topics, all summarized down to 3-4 pages. Most good business books are based on a handful of strong ideas, and then fill pages of copy with examples, analysis, the author's further opinion, etc. Why not capture that one strong idea in a couple summarized pages, then move on? Each week, ExecuBooks (a feature of a service called aheadSpace) adds another new release to their library. Summaries are available in various formats for easy reading on the go, or print-outs via PDF for your commute.

"Best of the Best" summaries from blogs: Many blogs feature regular "links" posts, which summarizes their take on great related blogging from across the blogosphere. I regularly count on these bloggers to do the heavy-lifting and deep-reading for me, then just scan their summaries for stories I might want to read more about. Blogs in general are a great way to allow other people (with more time) to do your reading for you, but these "best of" posts are like a lightning-round. Some blogs with particularly good summaries are MicroPersuasion (for media/marketing/PR news), LifeHacker (for productivity best practices) and WiseBread (for great personal finance advice).

What have I missed? What services and tools do you count on to summarize news and important information for you?

Two Minutes or Less?
Do It Now

When I think about procrastination, I think first of bigger projects. I have a column to write, a proposal to finish, a report to publish.

The real time-suckers are the much smaller projects. If you read an email and *don't* take action right away, you're procrastinating. If you see an interesting article or blog post and don't do something with it right away, you're delaying action – and you're procrastinating.

I fight this type of mini-procrastination all the time. It doesn't mean I have to actually *do* everything right then and there. It just means I need to *decide* what to do, and move on.

But if the task takes two minutes or less (respond to an email, set up a meeting, quickly scan an article), I try to do it right away. With such a short time period required for action, delaying that activity (and reviewing the request or task again later) is pure wasted time. Add that time up across a day of emails, blog posts, phone calls, etc. and it's a ton of wasted time.

Simply acting on those two-minutes-or-less tasks right away will work wonders to clear your inbox, get things done and keep you moving more productively throughout the day.

NOTES

NOTES

NOTES

~~~~~~~~~~~~~~~~~~~~~~~~~~~~~~~~~~~~~~

Messaging &
Customer Focus

~~~~~~~~~~~~~~~~~~~~~~~~~~~~~~~~~~~~~~

**Selling Value & Creating Preference
in a Commodity Business**

I was asked recently how to successfully sell value in a commodity business. When your product or service is virtually identical to what is available elsewhere, how do you create differentiation, preference, value and market share acceleration?

It's not easy, but there are ways. Here are five to start:

1. **Service:** How well you treat your customers can make a big difference, especially if you want to be a premium-priced commodity seller. Customers who don't value service will always buy on price, and if you want to be the low-cost leader, that's fine too. But if you want to sell value with a commodity, provide excellent, remarkable service at every level and every interaction with your customers and prospects.

2. **Trust:** What's your reputation? What are you known for? Do customers trust you, and why? Know what your customers value, and establish a tight bond between those values and the trust you create and strengthen in the way you do business, every day.

3. **The Little Things:** There are countless ways to do little, remarkable things for your customers. Unexpected things that make you stand out, thoughtful gestures that show you're different, and that you care. Real estate agents who bring new buyers a pizza or sandwiches on moving day, that's special. Auto dealerships that offer free car wash service for life. Things like that can be huge for differentiation and preference, not to mention word-of-mouth for your business to new prospective customers.

4. **A Consultative Approach to Selling:** Are you just selling the commodity, or are you providing additional value in the sale? Are you teaching customers more about the industry they work in, the environment in which they need that commodity. Are you helping them be more successful in the process of buying? Provide that kind of value-added service as part of the sale, and you're creating immediate value and differentiation.

5.   **Results:** A commodity market doesn't necessarily mean that every option is the same, and will deliver the same results. How are you able to transcend what you're selling, and deliver differentiation and value in how that commodity impacts your customers? Is the end-result better through you? How? And how effectively can you communicate that results-based differentiation? Let your happy customers tell that story for you. Use their enthusiasm and success in the market to drive preference and value.

 ## Are You Selling or Enabling? Adding Value beyond the Sale

Which way do you sell? Do you sell what you do? Or do you sell what your customers will do? Do you sell what your product does? Or do you sell what it's *going to do* for your customers?

Those are different things, of course.

Do you sell what the product looks like today? Or do you sell what your customer's business will look like after using that product? Finally, do you sell what you sell and that's all? Or do you also help your customers to be as successful as possible with what you're selling?

Actively teach your customers how to get more value, drive more results, and see greater success with your product? Use this approach - which starts well before customers buy - to become not just a seller but a trusted partner to your customers.

It's the essence of solutions-based selling, and it keeps going well after the purchase agreements are complete. This quote from Dunlop Tires CIO Dennis Courtney sums it up well:

"The products that a supplier offers are only a small part of the equation. Generally we could get what we need from several places, so it's not unique. These suppliers who try to sell the product - who try to show us their stuff is better - are missing the point. What we're looking for goes beyond the product. We're looking for business understanding, we're looking for whether they can adapt to our special needs or whether they can advise and help us. We want their salespeople to add something worthwhile on their own account."

When you sell, are you adding value before and beyond the sale?

Starting With Why

Too many sales and marketing messages, unfortunately, talk about "what" and "how". And at the front of the sales process, that's a shame. You're proud of what you've built, which is great. You have six new features in the latest version, awesome. But if you lead with a description of *what* you're selling, or *how* it works, you're skipping the most important part of the conversation.

Why the customer cares.

When you write about *why*, you're addressing your customer's world. You're speaking their language, feeling their pain, building credibility by associating with the challenges they face. Those challenges, that pain, are what drive demand for your product or service. It's why people buy.

If your prospect doesn't have that need, or you haven't established or created that need, selling the prospect on *what* you have and *how* it works isn't going to help. You've done nothing to build value, and given the prospect no context for which to understand why they need to talk to you in the first place.

In the end, it all comes down to *why*. Yes, you may eventually get to a product demo and operational training of how to get started.

But the top of the funnel is all about *why*.

How to Build Thought Leadership & Influence

The steps to building trust and credibility with a growing network is *relatively* straightforward:

1. Engage new contacts somewhere, based on *their* needs

2. Provide some immediate value, based on the messages/ competencies you want to represent

3. Establish a great first impression and initial reputation for those same messages/competencies

4. Continue passively reiterating that value/message through high-volume, high-leverage channels

Contacts in, influencers and pipeline out. The more you can start the process by reaching multiple contacts at once, the more efficient the model. If you have to engage people 1:1 at the start of the process, for example, it doesn't scale well. If you can engage folks via speaking engagements, third-party published articles, attending well-targeted networking events, etc., you get lots of input into the process at once.

How you choose to execute the "passive reiterating" depends on what channels your audience uses most, and which you're most comfortable with. Blogs, newsletters, Twitter, whatever. Could be just one, could be a couple, definitely doesn't need to be all.

Thinking about it this way is a bit systematic and perhaps cold, but it works as long as the content and value you're providing the individuals on the other side of the process is genuine, authentic and truly helpful.

 ## Build Brand & Sell More with Effective Storytelling

Marketing has become more analytical than ever. We have at our disposal an incredible amount of measurement tools to evaluate the success, profitability and ROI of our efforts.

But those metrics can be a slippery slope. It's really easy to focus so much on the metrics, that you forget the creative. Focus so much on identifying the opportunity gaps, that your strategy for approaching customers in that gap is an afterthought.

I was reminded of this when I heard Jon Rimmerman from *Garagiste* talking about storytelling. Jon started *Garagiste* to sell wine to his friends. His business? He sends emails talking about wine. If you want some, you reply with how many you want.

You can't buy wine on his Web site. His emails do not feature photos of the wine bottles. His emails tell stories about the wine - where it came from, its history, and not just how it tastes but *what it's like to taste it*.

Jon says the last thing on his mind when he writes his emails (which nearly

100,000 customers receive every weekday) is selling. Instead, he wants to tell a story. He wants to help the stressed-out executive take five minutes to relax and take a mental journey with him to Italy, or France, or Spain every day.

In the process, Jon sells a LOT of wine. A little less than $30 million a year worth, largely from telling stories.

Storytelling as an effective marketing tool is everywhere. Trader Joe's is another excellent example. While their competitors flood the market with full-color newspaper inserts that feature nothing more than photos and prices, Trader Joe's publishes the *Fearless Flyer*. Here's their own description of what it is:

The Fearless Flyer has been likened to a cross between Consumer Reports and Mad Magazine. We're not sure who said that, but we think they pretty much got it right. The Fearless Flyer is kind of like a newsletter, a catalog and a bit of a comic book all at the same time. It's our chance to give you loads of interesting (hopefully) information about our products. And along the way, we like to toss in some witty (we try) tidbits and even a few old-fashioned cartoons.

Trader Joe's has created an intensely loyal following, with a unique set of products and unique marketing that focuses almost entirely on storytelling. It's different, evokes the customer's imagination, and it's effective.

All of us can do a better job telling stories - stories about our products, our brands, our customers. Math and analytics tee up the opportunity. To convert, you have to start talking, and what you say is as important as how you say it.

☑ Trust Goes Both Ways (Why Consistency is Important)

Micah Baldwin from Lijit Networks gave the shortest presentation from 2009's Gnomedex, but it was arguably the most important for marketers. In just 10 minutes, he inspired more ideas and note-taking than many of the subsequent hour-long talks.

Among many topics, Micah talked about trust. His definition of trust is simple:

"Trust is the creation of an expectation that person A will always act as Person B expects them to act."

In other words, trust is your reputation when consistency is added to the equation. If your customers have come to expect you'll be honest and transparent in your dealings with them, you've established a very good kind of trust.

Based on Micah's definition, however, you can also establish bad trust. If you're always late, consistently overpromise and under deliver, or generally get defensive when someone questions your work, that's trust as well. Just not the trust you want to have earned.

So, if creating trust is about expectations and consistency, what does that mean for your business or brand? How are you accelerating and maintaining trust by ensuring a consistent experience for every customer, every time?

The bigger your business, the more difficult this will be. But the bigger your business, the more important consistency and trust will be to future growth, revenue and success.

✓ Are You Really Listening to Your Buyers?

RainToday recently published a study focused on the problems buyers encounter when choosing a new professional service provider. The full report is worth a quick read via their Web site (www.raintoday.com).

Particularly interesting was a chart indicating the specific problems buyers encounter when engaged in the sales process. The top reasons boil down to salesmanship. The *number one* problem buyers encounter (nearly 4 of 10 buyers) is that the salesperson "did not listen to me."

These were followed by 30% of buyers indicating that the seller did not respond to requests in a timely manner, and did not understand their needs.

These are clearly problems that every sales and marketing organization can address. Today.

At the very bottom of the list of buyer problems? Web site. Just 6% of buyers reported that information on and professionalism of the seller's Web site was a problem. With so many organizations spending tons of time and money fixing Web sites with the assumption that it has a significant impact on buyer perception and interest, this relatively low percentage should at least give marketers pause to possibly reconsider where their time is best spent to accelerate closed business.

Buyers want you to listen. To respond quickly. To understand what they need.

What could you do with your sales organization *today* to address and improve these issues?

☑ Joining, Talking & Participating

Want credibility with a set of prospective customers? Want to be accepted as one of them, as a part of their tribe?

It takes more than just joining their club. It takes more than just speaking their language, and talking at them.

To be accepted today, you have to participate.

Participation means two-way communication, in an authentic manner, on a regular basis. It takes more time, more effort, and more investment than what we used to be able to do – buy a list, get some PR, write a letter. In other words, talk *at* the prospect.

Today, prospects require and expect more. If you talk at them (in a letter, a blog post, an article in a trade publication), they expect to be able to talk and comment back. And then, in turn, they expect you to read their response and engage yet again.

It's more work. And as long as your prospects keep responding, it doesn't really end. But isn't that awesome?

The companies you want as your customers aren't just reading your stuff anymore. They're responding, engaging, asking you questions, questioning your opinions. They're getting to know you, and by participating back, you're earning their trust and respect. And if you keep participating, you can earn their business too.

NOTES

NOTES

NOTES

~~~~~~~~~~~~~~~~~~~~~~~~~~~~~~~~~~

Prospecting

~~~~~~~~~~~~~~~~~~~~~~~~~~~~~~~~~~

Lead Generation Modeling Made Simple

Too many marketers don't model how many leads they actually need to hit their organization's sales goal. Those who do model often overdo it.

But you've got to do the math. Most of the time it boils down to answering just two questions:

- How many opportunities are required to get a sale?

- How many leads do you need to create a new opportunity?

Let's leave out sales cycle length for now, to keep things simple. Let's just look at leads-to-opportunities-to-sales.

To build the model, you need a handful of inputs:

- Average sales price of a closed deal

- % of leads that turn into a new sales opportunity

- % of new sales opportunities that convert into a sale

- Average cost per lead

If you don't know these figures explicitly, come up with a reasonable, but somewhat conservative guess. With this input, you can build a model telling you:

- How many leads you need

- How many sales will result (and with what bookings output)

- How much those sales will cost via a paid lead generation campaign

And with that model, if the inputs are isolated and the lead/opportunity/sales figures are calculated with simple formulas, you can make adjustments to the inputs to see what the sales and/or revenue impact would be if you:

- Generated more leads

- Increased the average sales price

- Increased the % of leads you can close

- Increased the % of opportunities you can close

Start simple, but build this model and share it with your team. Discuss it with sales management. Get on the same page, and execute with more confidence that what you're doing is leading directly to sales success.

 ## Stop Making It Harder For Customers to Engage & Buy

At this year's Super Bowl, only a couple ads included a specific and trackable call to action (including Dockers, whose site immediately went down in the minutes after their spot aired), and none that I could see referenced anything on Facebook, Twitter or any other social network.

With a significant percent of Super Bowl viewers simultaneously on their computers, and a further opportunity to engage customers and prospects well after their 30-seconds-of-fame, I was surprised to see that in 2010 so few advertisers specifically invite viewers to continue the conversation.

Shortly after the Super Bowl, Expedia brand manager Julie Lowe gave a good explanation at a Super Bowl Ad Replay event I attended:

"Big companies that spend money on Super Bowl ads have too many different and separated marketing groups, with not enough communication and coordination between them. The brand or advertising teams likely managed the Super Bowl strategy largely on their own, without thinking about integrating efforts from the social media or direct teams that sit next to them."

Your company or marketing department may be organized into functional groups, but your customer doesn't think that way. Today's increasingly multi-tasking customer requires a different way of operating, and a new level of cross-platform integration from marketers.

Your company just spent three million dollars on thirty seconds of air time. Why not capture more value than that?

Of course, most of us aren't running those kinds of ads. But how well does your marketing today take into account the multi-faceted ways customers want to interact with you and each other? How easy are you making it for them to engage, share, participate - and buy?

 ## The Three Things You Must Know Before Any Marketing Campaign

We often get approached by companies that want us to help them execute marketing campaigns. They need help with copy for their emails, ideas for their new print advertising or suggestions for how to get the most out of an upcoming trade show.

But before we can be smart about helping new clients drive sales and revenue from these tactics, we have to take a quick step back and ensure three things are understood and put into perspective:

1. **Your Customers:** Who are they? What are their core needs, objectives, pain points? What gets them fired up in the morning, and what keeps them up at night? What (and who) influences and motivates them?

    The more you understand your customer, the better your marketing will be. And frankly, if you don't know your customer well, I'm not sure how you can put a successful product into play in the first place.

    Don't feel like you know enough about your customers? Just ask! Take a list of customers and call them. Don't pitch them, but ask them about their business, their needs, their pain. You'll learn a ton.

    Your front-line employees are hearing from customers every day. Your customer service reps, sales team, account managers - they all are a wealth of knowledge about your customers if you're willing to ask and listen.

2. **Your Products:** What you're selling needs to closely align with the needs of your customers. It needs to clearly fill a need, solve a problem or provide a benefit that can be easily communicated.

    Too many companies describe their products to customers by explaining features. That's a mistake, especially at the front of the conversation and sales cycle. To gain the customer's attention, you have to speak in terms of benefits. Don't talk about the how and what. Address the why.

And when building and updating products, ensure that the customer's voice is close by throughout. Product plans and specs are often built directly from customer feedback, but that customer closeness can get lost as decisions are made to get the product launched. Don't let that happen on your watch.

3. **Your Objectives:** Even if you understand your customers well, and have a product that directly aligns with the customer's needs, there are a million ways to take that message to market. There are countless customer segments, marketing channels and likely several different product and/or service lines on which you can focus.

    Which are most important? What combination will most directly lead to success for your organization this year? If you've defined goals for the organization, and broken that down to a handful of focus areas or "bets" in the marketplace, that gives your marketing the direction it needs to focus on the right customers, the right channels and the right products.

    Now you have clear direction from your customers, your products and your organizational objectives. Doesn't that make marketing execution easier, and much more likely to succeed?

 ## Five Fast Steps to Better Relations (& Results) Between Sales & Marketing

Too often, sales and marketing blame each other for a lack of results. The leads aren't good. Sales doesn't follow up. The excuses go on and on.

If this sounds familiar for your organization, there are things you can start doing right away to mend fences and start on a path towards not only better relations, but far better revenue results.

Call a sales and marketing summit, and don't let anyone leave the room until the following five things are agreed upon:

1. **Common lead definitions:** What, exactly, is a qualified lead? What are its characteristics? Get as detailed as you need to be, but make

sure both sales and marketing agree on that definition. That way, when leads are delivered to sales, they at minimum meet the basic criteria you've both agreed on to make them worth the sales team's time for follow-up.

2. **Initial response time:** If the leads are good (and meet the minimum qualified definition), you need a "service agreement" for how quickly those leads will get their first response. If the lead is waiting for something (a white paper, for instance) response time should likely be no longer than 24 business hours. In other cases, 48 hours may be acceptable. Decide what's right for your organization and customer, get sales management's buy-in, communicate it clearly to the sales team and put in place reporting tools to make it super-easy to track this on a daily basis (and send both you and the sales rep alerts when leads fall outside of the service agreement).

3. **Lead follow-up steps and channels:** How many times should a lead be attempted before the sales rep gives up and moves on? Should all of those attempts be via phone, or should there be a mix of other channels – email, social media channels, in-person, etc.? If you don't reach agreement on this critical process, every sales rep will have his own idea of what's right. Some will call once, leave a message, and consider the lead dead. Others will call the poor prospect 20 times. Create a standard with sales not only to ensure leads are thoroughly vetted, but also to ensure sales is moving on to fresher opportunities if there's nobody at home.

4. **Clear lead stages:** A lead comes in. The rep starts to attempt a call back. She reaches the lead and determines it's a good prospect, or long-term prospect, or just not qualified. How does she report this information to you? What lead stages have you set up in your lead management or CRM system to not only make it easy and clear how you want sales to categorize their working leads, but also to report to management progress and quality of leads (not to mention improve your lead generation ROI performance moving forward)? Don't go overboard – 15 lead stages gets way too complicated – but 4-6 stages are reasonable and actionable for most sales environments.

5. **Handing leads back to marketing:** According to *MarketingSherpa* and others, the vast majority of leads generated by B2B organizations in particular will buy – just not right now. Those leads (once they're identified as such) need to be passed back to marketing for active nurturing. Make sure there's a clear process for sales to do just that – ideally with the click of a button.

Five Tips to Avoid Call Reluctance & Reach New Prospects

Most sales professionals hate cold calling. Following up with existing leads sometimes isn't much better or easier. Even the best salespeople often have a strong case of call reluctance that's difficult to shake.

But once successful salespeople get rolling, they often find it easy to keep that momentum and generate results – live contacts, interested prospects, new sources of closeable pipeline.

Here are five ways to get past that case of call reluctance and get more of your leads moving towards a sale.

1. **Script the first 30 seconds:** Oftentimes call reluctance comes from a concern that the beginning of a conversation may be awkward. Get past that fear by writing down, visualizing and even practicing the first 20-30 seconds of the call. Have a specific script you will use printed out and next to your phone. It'll give you confidence that each call will be easier to warm up, and get right to the conversation you want to be having.

2. **Have a great voicemail script ready:** Let's face it, most of the calls you make will result in a voicemail. Many sales pros leave a long, rambling voicemail with no direction, no urgency and no call to action. Have a great voicemail script ready beforehand, and use it every time. Leave something that's no longer than 40-45 seconds, had a good pace, a sense of urgency, and a strong offer or call to action to get your prospect to call back quickly. When you have a voicemail script like this, that you know works, it's easier and faster to get through more of your calls (because you *know* those prospects will be calling back).

3. **Turn off all other distractions:** You've done it too – you make the first couple calls, get a kernel of momentum, then check your email or Facebook page and it's all gone. When you're ready to make those calls, turn off everything – email, your Web browser, RSS feeds, notifications, everything. Get yourself into a zone where you're making those calls and nothing else. You'll be surprised how quickly you get through the list, and drive results for yourself.

4. **Get momentum, and keep going:** On a related note, have a strong list to call and keep going until you're through it. Do it at a set time, perhaps the same time of the day every day, and make sure those around you know you're staying focused. And tell your manager. Staying focused can take discipline, even if you don't have distractions. You leave a couple good voicemails, maybe have a good conversation that moves a prospect along, and you want to get some more coffee. Avoid these things, and make the next call.

5. **Do it early, or do it late:** When you first get into the office in the morning, make those calls. There won't be fire drills, you won't know what's awaiting you in your email, and you're more likely to get call-backs later that day from the voicemails you've left in the morning. Next best strategy is to schedule those calls late in the day. After 4:00, you're more likely to catch your prospect in their office, doing their own catch-up before leaving for the day. You'll either reach more people live, or leave voicemails that will be returned first-thing the next day (getting your *next* sales day off to a great start).

 ## Social Lead Generation

Let's face it, the term "social media" doesn't mean much. It's passive, and speaks more to the channel vs. the intent or objective of what's actually happening there.

Your customers are talking to each other. They always have. Only now, they have tools to do it faster, in real-time, and in front of everybody else. That's social media.

But social media, as we know it now, is really the new PR. It's your best channel to reach prospective customers in their current environment. You have less control than you used to, sure, but make no mistake – social media is at the top of your sales funnel.

So let's stop calling it social media, and start calling it social lead generation. At least amongst ourselves.

Today's buyers are presenting themselves to you like never before. They're sharing their interests, their needs, their feelings, their pain. They're telling you, in front of everybody else (including your competitors), exactly what they want.

It's a perfect opportunity to meet them, engage them, earn their trust and respect, and give them exactly what they're asking for.

That's social lead generation.

Don't treat it like lead generation. That runs the risk of ruining its authenticity. But as a core component of building credibility, attention and respect for your products and services, know that – in the end – what you do with this opportunity is measured by its value in engaging and creating new customers.

How to Find Your Customers & Prospects on Twitter

A good way to do this with prospects or an industry in general is to think about the keywords they would likely include in their Twitter bio. Then use one of a number of Twitter search tools to determine which Twitter users have those keywords in their current bios. It's not exact, but gives you a ballpark.

For example, if you're targeting contractors and home services professionals, search for Twitter users using keywords such as "landscaping", "remodeler", "home stager", and the like. You probably already have a sense for the overall universe of said practitioners in a given market, so this can give you a rough ballpark of prospective customer penetration on Twitter.

Easiest way to do the same with current customers you have is to ask them! If you have customer service reps or account managers, have them ask the question at the end of inbound calls. Ask for it on registration forms for upcoming customer events. Or if you want to be more aggressive, include a pop-up or other request form when they next log in or visit your Web site.

Give some examples of the kind of value-added content you tweet about so they're more driven to sign up. Your customers will want you to follow them too, so they'll be happy to pass along their Twitter account name.

☑ How to Build a List of Your Competitor's Customers

To gain market share, of course, you either need to bring new customers into the category, or get existing category customers to switch from your competitors.

Switching customers can oftentimes be faster and easier, as you don't need to sell the customer on the need for the category in general - just that your product is better, faster, cheaper or more effective.

Getting your hands on that competitor's customer list is another story.

But in today's world of empowered consumers armed with a plethora of online social communication tools, seeking out your competitor's customers may be easier than you think. True, getting the complete list may be next to impossible, but here are some tips for finding who's using "the other guys", and which of them might be ripe for a switch:

- **Set up a Twitter search** for your competitor's name and product/brand names. You'll still need to sort through the press announcements and employee tweets to find the customers, but I guarantee they're there. Some are actively complaining. That's where to start.

- **Do similar searches in LinkedIn,** specifically in the Groups and Answers sections. Same thing - figure out where customers and/or users in your category assemble, and find those who are talking about their experiences with your competitors.

- **Actively seek, search and participate in blogs and discussion groups** that attract customers discussing issues (general or specific) related to your category.

Trolling and pulling prospects may be a quick way to use these channels to find "switcher" business, but each channel also represents a fantastic opportunity to engage the broader community of users and participants with your own brand, content and offers.

Simply starting a conversational presence in these places (to build credibility, not just to sell) is an easy and cost-effective way to directly target both an immediate and long-term stream of prospective new customers.

Do you have examples of successful switcher campaigns from the channels above, or other competitor list-finding best practices? What are you doing to actively find, engage and convince your category's other customers to switch to you?

 ## B2B Lead Generation: Four Better Measures of Success

If you work for or with a marketing team that drives leads for a sales team, it's likely a mistake to measure your success based on lead volume.

Lead volume doesn't matter.

What matters, of course, is revenue. Your job as a marketer is to give your sales team the best opportunities possible to close business, increase sales and grow the value of the overall business. To that effect, there are far better ways to measure marketing success instead of pure leads. Here are four I like in particular:

1. **Lead quality:** Leads are only good if they represent individuals or companies who can buy. Sit down with your sales team and agree on a common definition for a qualified lead. This can include things like company size, title, industry, purchase timeline - whatever you agree on. Leads you generate that aren't quite "in profile" aren't necessarily bad - some will still have revenue in them - but your primary job is to focus on optimizing volume and cost of the in-profile leads first.

2. **Pipeline contribution:** Simply put, how many of those leads generated become active sales opportunities? Sure, this step requires work by your sales team, but it's another good indicator of lead quality. This step also requires marketing to work collaboratively with sales to get the job done. No more passing leads over the wall and walking away. Marketing's job includes helping the sales team continue working with new prospects until they're ready to buy.

3. **Deal size:** If you look deep into your lead generation metrics, I guarantee you'll find trends that help you increase deal size at the lead level. Do particular industries buy more? Do certain titles tend to buy more products? Certain company sizes? Geographies? Find the trends that lead to bigger deals, and find ways to generate more leads like that moving forward.

4. **% and # of deals from nurture database:** If a lead isn't ready to buy, but hasn't said no, it's marketing's job to nurture that prospect until it's ready to be passed back to sales. How well does your marketing team drive interest and urgency with your nurture database? How well does marketing identify when nurtured prospects are ready to buy? This is a great way to ensure your marketing team is innovating ways to drive urgency among your prospect database, and many of those urgency drivers will work in primary lead generation channels and campaigns as well.

Last but not least, there's of course cost per lead *all the way through to the sale*. Too many B2B marketers measure cost per lead (and sometimes even cost per in-profile lead), but fail to look at relative marketing cost of the opportunity and sale. A certain lead source can look great based on cost per lead, but if the conversion to opportunity and sale (not to mention lifetime value) is too low, leads that cost more can actually be better for the business after sale price and renewals are factored in.

What success measures work for your marketing team to drive focus on revenue?

 ## Reaching New Customers with LinkedIn Groups

LinkedIn's relevance not only as a professional networking tool but as an active social media marketing tool is increasing at a rapid rate. Among the various ways to network and reach customers on LinkedIn, the Groups feature offers significant, measurable opportunity for smart companies.

In a nutshell, LinkedIn Groups are opt-in sets of individuals who share a common interest. There's an extremely long tail of groups on LinkedIn, covering a wide variety of subject matter. Chances are whatever market you're in or product/service you're selling, there are at least a handful of groups on LinkedIn focused on it.

They may not all have thousands of members, but these individuals each represent not only a prospective customer, but an influencer who can reach others in their own networks – beyond the confines of the specific online group.

Using these groups to grow your own business won't work immediately. This isn't direct marketing with immediate response and revenue, at least not likely. To benefit from these groups, to provide value to other members and earn their confidence, respect and business, you need to take the time to become a respected, valued member of the community.

But with time and focus, LinkedIn Groups can deliver thought leadership, new customers and even new brand ambassadors for your business. Here are a few recommended steps to get started.

- **Join relevant groups:** Do several wide searches in the Groups section to see what's available and relevant to you, and your business. Don't think like a marketer or salesperson, think like a customer (and you're the customer). Where can you provide value? For which groups do you have something constructive to add (not just a sales pitch)? Those are the groups where organic participation will be easier and more effective from you.

- **Post articles of interest:** Start building a presence for yourself in the group by posting articles of interest. Do not post articles from your own site or blog, at least not initially. Build credibility with the group and for yourself by offering purely educational and value-added content from across the Web that other members will appreciate. These articles will not only appear on the group home page, but also in email digests sent to the majority of members.

- **Participate in discussions:** Look for questions you can answer, or questions worth introducing to the discussion board. Be educational, and do not sell. Recommend ideas, solutions, other services or products beyond what you directly offer.

- **Reach out to individual members:** Once a member of a group, LinkedIn gives you the ability to send and receive direct messages from other members without either party revealing their direct contact information. If you see comments in the discussion board that could use a direct vs. group response, use this feature to contact the individual member. This is a great way to start building an individual relationship with a member who may be a good sales prospect, but do so based on providing value and earning trust.

- **Invite your customers to participate:** The best way to start introducing your product or service into these groups is not through you directly, but through your customers. Invite a handful of your customers to join the LinkedIn Group with you. Their engagement with other members on a variety of topics will give them the credibility to – when the time and context is right – introduce and recommend your product.

 ## Best Practices for Successful Lead Generation Webinars

The use of Webinars to engage prospective customers and generate leads has increased exponentially over the past year. As such, best practices for making them successful for lead generation have become clear. Here are several recommendations for planning and executing Webinars that develop thought leadership for your business, and qualified leads for your sales team.

PLANNING

- **Have a bias for action:** Get in there and get started. Don't worry about getting hundreds of prospects on the call. Don't worry about making everything perfect. No matter how much time you spend planning, your first couple Webinars will be a learning experience. Know your audience, know your content and get out there and start executing.

- **Pick the right day and time:** Customize this based on when your audience is most likely to be available. For example, don't plan on reaching sales professionals at the end of the month, or accounting targets at the start of a new month. Avoid Mondays and Fridays. 1:00pm East/10:00am Pacific time is a generally good time (avoid lunch on both coasts).

- **Scan for existing conflicts:** Before locking in your day and time, check to make sure there aren't existing conferences, holidays or other Webinars planned for the same audience at the same day and time.

- **Choose a third-party speaker:** Even if the topics you've chosen are well-known to employees, pick someone outside the company to give the presentation. It'll come across far more credibly if it's seen as "independent", and you'll likely get a higher registration rate by further separating the content from your sales pitch.

- **Ask for content feedback from registrants:** As you register attendees, ask them for specific up-front questions or requests based on your general topic. For example, if you're doing a Webinar on health care reform for HR professionals, ask them what specific questions they have. As you see patterns in their answers, you'll know how to customize your content and presentation to make it even more relevant.

EXECUTION

- **Teach, don't preach:** Everything about an effective Webinar should be value-added to the audience. Make sure they walk away with knowledge, insights and specific ideas that can help them - both immediately and long-term. As such, make your content easy to digest. Top 10 lists are great - easy to follow along and easy to pull next steps from.

- **Don't demo:** Unless you've promoted the Webinar explicitly as an online demo of your product or service, don't spent time showing much of the product. Your product should be a natural next step to what you've presented. If your content has set up and addressed the problem, the pain, the challenge or the current situation your customers are in, it will intensify the need for what you're selling. If your Webinar content is done well, it will organically drive more attendees to want to see what you can offer to help them.

- **Be interactive:** Change the format, the speaker, the visuals on a regular basis to keep your viewers engaged. If you have a specific guest speaker, consider presenting in a Q&A format so that different people are speaking. This change in voice will keep people following. Consider also interjecting video or other visual tools in between slides.

- **Ask qualifying questions:** Use your Webinar service's polling feature to ask questions within the Webinar. You can use these answers to customize follow-on content, ensure what you're addressing is reaching and resonating with viewers, and also qualify attendees as leads for post-event follow-up.

- **Be ready for the Q&A:** At the end of a good Webinar, attendees can ask questions. But sometimes they need to be warmed up. Have a few "canned" questions ready to address "from the audience" right away. Believe me; this will help other attendees feel comfortable raising their own hands with more questions.

FOLLOW-UP

- **Treat registrants the same as attendees:** To a large extent, whether or not the registrant actually attended the live event isn't important. What's more important is that they resonated enough with the topic to register and put it on their calendar. That relevance means they likely have a need for the content (and solution) you're offering. Everyone who registers for your Webinar (not just the 55% who actually attend) can be a good prospect.

- **Follow up quickly:** Don't let those leads go more than three days without a follow-up call. Make the follow-up value-added as well. Ensure the content was valuable, ask if they have additional questions, offer an "additional" article, white paper or other content related to the topic.

- **Make materials available for free:** Provide the slides, notes, transcript, etc. to attendees, registrants and anyone else for free. Put it on *SlideShare*, post it on your blog, make it as easy to access and pass along as possible.

- **Conduct and record a post-mortem:** What went well? What could have gone better? Capture this information quickly (ideally the same day as the Webinar) to ensure you're improving the next time.

How to Profitably Generate Leads & Sales from Trade Shows

Trade shows represent the marketing channel sales and marketing people everywhere love to hate. High costs, LOTS of time (before and during the event), typically followed by less-than-exciting leads and few converted sales.

But as much as I also typically shy away from trade shows as a front-line marketing channel for demand generation, they do have their place in delivering solid, profitable revenue. You just have to get a few things right. This list is by no means exhaustive, but it's a start in the right direction.

- **Pre-show expectations:** First and foremost, make sure you understand what trade shows can do, and what they likely cannot do. Trade shows are busy, attendees are scattered and flustered on the show floor, so having a lot of high-quality conversations that lead to short-term revenue isn't likely the expectation you want to set. Fast deals are bluebirds, with the majority of attendees earlier in the buying cycle which means a longer lead time to being ready for your sales pipeline. Most trade show revenue, therefore, will be long term. Go into the show with that mindset and you're already a step ahead.

- **Establish and estimate required ROI:** Before going any further, do the napkin math to make sure your fully-burdened spend (including out-of-pocket budget, travel costs, as well as the opportunity cost of the team's time) is worth the expected sales. Know up front, before the show is green-lighted, whether it has a chance of being a profitable effort, ideally with an expectation of exactly how many sales need to come directly from attendees. More often than not, this ROI will either keep you from wasting further time on a show that's destined to be a failure, or at minimum will give you guidance on the investment and strategy required to make it a success.

- **Pre-show buzz and "appointments":** Get a copy of the attendee list if possible, and give expected booth visitors - before they're inundated with messages at the show - a reason to stop by. This is where knowing your audience and their pain points well can make it easy to map that knowledge to an offer or message that prioritizes a trip to your booth over others. If they plan for it, they're more likely to not only stop by but invest a little more time in your presentation.

- **How you approach prospects:** At the show itself, how do you engage traffic? How do you get browsers to break their gait, pause in front of your booth and engage with your staff? The answer is likely not a cheap giveaway or in-booth game. What message or offer can your booth staff deliver in three seconds or less to a passing attendee that will get at least 50% of them to stop? It's likely something related to your value proposition - a sample, a no-risk trial, or even a challenge. These types of offers will likely generate the most visitors and better prospects.

- **After-show follow-up:** Sadly, this step is ignored, forgotten or just plain dropped by many sales and marketing teams. But it's arguably the most important step of all. You've just invested a significant amount of time and money to capture sales leads early in their purchase cycle. At the show itself, they were overwhelmed with messages. And few of the other exhibitors will do anything coordinated to follow up. Think in advance, before you attend the show, what you want your follow-up to look like. Whether it's all from marketing, or combined with some sales team follow-up directly, plan for this in advance so your team can hit the ground running as soon as the show is over. Even if you decide to give attendees a day or two to get home first, having this done beforehand will ensure the plan is well executed and measured.

- **Nurture, nurture, nurture:** Knowing these leads are early in their buying cycle; make sure they are added to your broader lead nurturing efforts. If you don't have one, come up with a plan that "touches" these leads on a regular basis with relevant information, messaging and offers to ensure you stay top of mind well after the show. If you made a good first impression at the booth, that's a great start. If you fail to follow up and build momentum on that early start after the show, your expected ROI will fall as well.

- **Track results regularly and long-term:** If you know going in that collected leads will likely take longer to close, you're less likely to deem the event a failure after just 30 days of follow-up. But no matter how long your sales cycle, measuring conversion and close results from collected leads is critical. If you're a Salesforce.com user, putting all collected leads into a unique Campaign is your best choice. But no matter what you use, have the patience and discipline to watch conversion over time.

Why I Still Use Business Cards

I'm hearing more and more people express pride over the fact that they no longer carry business cards, and consider the rest of us archaic for doing so. That feels a little short-sighted to me.

Would the world be more efficient if business cards no longer existed? I doubt it. I still consider business cards an important part of my networking and follow-up process.

As a business card recipient, that little piece of thin cardboard is a reminder that I met you, a reminder to follow-up, and the fastest way possible to – in the moment when we've met, wherever that context may be – get your contact information for future follow-up. Sure, it might be nicer to just "bump" your iPhones and transfer the contact information. But then it's too easy to forget to follow-up, forget that article I promised to send to you, etc.

In almost every context I can think of where I've met a new person, the last thing I want to do at that point is bury my nose in my laptop or smartphone and type someone's complete contact information, plus any next steps or to-do's based on that conversation. I can take care of that later, just grab a card and continue focusing on the individual, not their digits.

As a business card distributor, most of the world still asks for them. Yes, at technology events they might be waning in volume and impact. A little. But most of the rest of the world wants a card. If you don't have one to give them, you're missing out on any number of opportunities to network, get business or otherwise share mutually-beneficial information with that person – both now and down the road.

Do you still use business cards? Do you have an effective process for not only collecting and distributing them, but also processing them (the information and next steps) after you receive them?

✓ How to Integrate Social & Traditional Marketing

Companies are wondering how to not just build out their social media presence, but how to integrate it with the rest of their marketing strategy.

My advice? Stop thinking about them as two different things. Distinctions between social and "traditional" marketing are meaningless, or at least temporary. Why? Because your customer doesn't care.

Your customer doesn't differentiate between their social media time, their Internet time, their mobile time and then their "traditional" media time. In the real world, all of these experiences blend together, happen in rapid sequence and often happen simultaneously.

Your customer experiences all of these things at different times and possibly on different platforms, but their impression of you, your products and your brand is singular. Their awareness, preference and action towards what you're doing and selling is not divided between media platforms and marketing divisions.

Remember 10-12 years ago when your company created a separate Internet advertising department? Even that feels a little quaint now. Eventually, progressive brands realized that distinguishing between channels was contrary to the way their customers thought, created first and lasting impressions and made decisions. The same goes today for social media.

But if you're still faced with the reality of separate teams or efforts managing your social marketing from everything else, take a moment to step back, forget about your internal divisions for a moment, and think about the customer. What is she doing? How is she interacting with your brand, with those that influence her, and with the critical decision and touch points that compel her to make a purchase decision? How are you organizing your marketing strategy not by channel or platform, but by the purchase cycle she follows, as well as the information and sources she naturally gravitates towards at each stage of the research, discovery, preference, trial and purchase process?

I'm not saying you still don't have to integrate how you manage your marketing. I just think that when we talk about how to better manage cross-platform programs, perhaps we're starting with the wrong question.

☑️ Mapping How You Sell to How Your Customers Buy

Your customer started buying long before you started selling. And most of the time, your customer started buying before they even consciously *knew* they were buying.

Take real estate. Most real estate agents market their services to active home buyers and sellers. They're looking for people that want to buy or sell soon. But research has shown that buyers and sellers choose a real estate agent towards the *end* of their buying cycle, and that the cycle can last for two years overall.

That buying cycle doesn't start with looking for homes, researching neighborhoods, or talking to agents. It started with experiences. Getting tired of the long commute, feeling a little more crowded in the existing house with a couple kids, etc. That's the very beginning of what becomes the purchase of a new home.

At the beginning of every buying cycle are experiences. These experiences eventually become needs, gaps, pain. Those needs become a search for a solution.

Most companies create and manage a sales process based on the way they want to sell. Smart companies create a sales process based on how their customers buy. But even fewer companies build a sales and marketing strategy that reaches *way* back to the beginning of when the customer need, gap and pain materialize. That's when they start looking around, doing their own homework and educating themselves on the topic. And that's where you can build value.

Mapping how you sell to how your customers buy teaches you everything you need to know (and do) to build awareness, preference and demand to increase close rates and accelerate your own selling cycles.

You may already know a lot about your customers – what they do, what they need, how they work. But do you understand how they buy?

NOTES

NOTES

NOTES

Pipeline Strategy & Management

12 Tips for Building & Managing a Bigger Sales Pipeline

Whether you're managing sales for a large enterprise organization, or are trying to build business for your own one-man-shop, these tips should help guide your thinking, strategy and action for building and managing a bigger sales pipeline.

Why do you need a pipeline in the first place?

1. **Most leads aren't sales-ready:** Whether you're sending out campaigns or fielding inbound calls, as little as 15% of your leads are going to be both qualified and sales-ready. The majority of your leads may be qualified, but they're not ready to be worked into an active buying cycle. You need a pipeline that can triage and communicate with these prospects accordingly.

2. **You can't focus on everything:** You simply cannot keep everything in your head. Notebooks and post-its on your computer monitor aren't going to help either. You need a system to manage lead volume, status, next steps, reminders, etc. for you. Your time, right now, is best spent on the best prospects, ready to take the next step. Let your pipeline manage the rest of the work for you.

3. **The right message at the right time:** With every stage of the buying process, your prospects will want (and accept) different things from you. This includes type of information, frequency of contact and channel(s) used to communicate. By using a pipeline with defined stages, most of this thinking is already done for you. You simply execute.

4. **Maximum sales, minimal work:** An effective sales pipeline strategy will help you get the maximum sales and conversion from your prospects, while doing as little work as possible. It's not about being lazy or taking shortcuts, it's about working smarter and respecting your buyers. And it works.

How to approach your sales pipeline

5. **It's a pipeline, but your prospects shouldn't know that:** The last thing you want to do is make your prospects feel like they're in some kind of sales funnel. Don't treat them like a number, and don't force them to go faster than they're willing or ready to go. An effective sales pipeline will nurture prospects on their time with occasional offers to let them self-select into a more active communication and buying cycle

6. **DO NOT SELL:** Seriously, especially in the early stages when prospects aren't ready to buy. Instead - add value, educate, connect and empower. Become a trusted adviser for your prospects, someone they can trust, someone they know won't sell them something they don't need or that won't benefit them. The more you build value, the more your prospects will look forward to hearing from you

7. **Automate as much as you can:** This means reminders for next steps, the next steps themselves (based on activity triggers), content templates you can quickly customize for individual prospects, etc. Custom communication is important, but if you understand your customer base, there's plenty to templatize and automate to save you significant time and hassle as you execute.

8. **Differentiate from competitors:** As you build value and communicate with prospects all along the sales pipeline, also build differentiation and preference for you and your products/services. Don't slam competitors, and in most cases don't even address them directly. But make it clear how you're special, how you're different. Differentiation and preference will lead to action and decision in your favor.

Key strategies for effective pipeline execution

9. **Use a lead management system:** At minimum, make sure you have a CRM system that integrates contacts, accounts and sales opportunities in one place. Salesforce.com does a great job of this, but may be too much for small businesses. For smaller or early-stage organizations, I'd also recommend PipelineDeals or Highrise.

10. **Clearly define lead and opportunity stages:** Define not only the stages your prospects go through (from the very beginning, nurture stages through to the sale), but also define your communication strategy at each stage - what do they get, how often, in what format, etc. Defining this up front will make decisions and actions both faster and more successful as you execute (especially if you have a team where common definitions are critical).

11. **Focus on great content:** Be remarkable. Be educational. Make yourself required-reading for your prospects. Teach them how to do their jobs better, how to live their lives better. Great content, especially in today's information-overload world, can be a powerful differentiator and *attractor* of new business to you.

12. **Make it easy for prospects to move forward:** Give your prospects ample chances to "raise their hand" to move forward more actively into the buying stages. Create offers that inherently mean they're interested in moving forward - price estimator tools, free trials, buying guides, etc. Integrate these offers into your other content, putting the prospect in control of taking the next step. If you've done your work up front - building value, differentiation, preference - they'll come to you to buy far more often.

A Three-Step Process for Effective Sales Territory Planning

Great salespeople have a plan. They have a goal (quota and/or commission) and a specific written plan of how they're going to get there. Great salespeople do this on their own, but it's also a worthwhile exercise to ask your sales team to go through at the beginning of each selling period (especially if you're on quarterly or annual sales cycles).

It's far better to know, at the beginning of the month, quarter or year, your individual and overall level of confidence for hitting your number. If there's a gap in sales pipeline, or other obstacles in between you and your goal, it's better to know that now vs. the end of the quarter.

Smart salespeople look at this level of territory business planning not as a chore, but as a roadmap for how to prioritize their time - how and where they should be committing their own resources most effectively to close more business.

A good sales territory plan should answer three questions:
1.   What do I have?
2.   What am I going to do?
3.   What do I need?

You can do this by breaking down your expected closed business for the period into three parts:

1.   **Current pipeline:** What current opportunities do I have that are expected to close by the end of this selling period? Which do I have the most confidence in? Which might be a stretch but are still qualified and more than likely to close?

2.   **Leads:** What leads am I working with currently that are qualified and likely to become closed opportunities between now and the end of the selling period? These are more long-shots, perhaps, because they're not as far along. But you still have an expectation that they will close.

3.   **Proactive targets:** What are the additional accounts within my territory that I am going to proactively pursue and close by the end of this sales period? This section may constitute the "gap" between your quota and the combination of current pipeline and leads you're already managing, to give you a big enough pipeline to close and exceed your quota.

As a salesperson, you think first about what you can control. The above three categories put specific focus on what you have, and what you can still do. But there still may be significant roadblocks, obstacles or needs for opportunities within any of these three areas to get them closed. This is where a good territory plan specifically identifies these needs, at the start of the selling period, as "asks" for others in your organization - your manager, marketing, the product team, an executive, etc.

As the salesperson, you are the quarterback of the deal. It's your job to leverage whatever resources are available to you within (or even outside) of the organization to help your prospect reach a decision. Your territory plan is a great place to identify specific needs tied to potential new business, which gives the context and motivation to others to help.

☑ Selling vs. Simmering: Knowing How & When to Close the Deal

The right buyers for your product or service need what you're selling. You represent a link between where they are today and where they want to be moving forward. They *want* to buy from you.

This applies, of course, to buyers that are not only qualified, but are *ready* to buy. The vast majority of qualified buyers just aren't there yet. According to a recent *MarketingSherpa* report, as little as 15% of sales leads are both qualified and ready to buy.

Smart sales organizations take a "selling vs. simmering" approach to their prospective customers. If the prospect is in an active buying cycle, they're ready to work with sales. The role of sales, in this context, isn't to sell as much as help the buyer buy what they already need.

Simmering is quite different. Simmering takes a qualified buyer that doesn't have an immediate need, and ensures that when they are ready to buy, the decision of whom to buy from is essentially already made. That means staying in touch on a regular basis, but purposefully *not* selling.

This takes patience, and discipline. When your sales manager is breathing down your neck to close more business this quarter, it's tempting to reach down to some of the prospects that are simmering and push them into a sale. But those prospects aren't ready to buy, and pushing them to move more quickly will not only decrease your conversion rates and waste your time, but will also put off the customer such that they may seek products or services (when they're ready to buy) from someone else.

Your best chance at getting the maximum sales output and conversion rate from the prospects in your pipeline is to know who's ready to buy now, and who needs more simmering.

☑ What Happens After the Lead?

Leads alone mean nothing.

Leads don't equal revenue. By definition, leads are just prospective buyers who haven't yet bought a thing.

Marketers get upset when their executives think of them, and their budgets, as a cost center. But those same marketers often focus on generating leads, and that's it. They don't hold themselves accountable for the sale.

What happens after the lead is what's really important. So you have someone who qualifies as a prospective buyer. Maybe that prospect has even shown interest, shared a pain that you can ease.

They still need to buy. They will still have objections. Some may buy on their own, but most need to be walked through the sale.

Smart marketers know that leads are just the beginning. They know that their job isn't really done until leads *buy*.

Successful marketers go beyond setting a common definition for qualified leads with their sales counterparts. They also work with sales to define stages of the sales process, and develop tools to help sales reps sell, and make it easier for buyers to buy.

The best B2B marketers think, work and execute like they're in sales, not marketing. Because your sales reps know that generating the lead is at the top of their funnel, not the bottom.

How to Achieve a Frictionless Sale Every Time

If you know your audience well, accurately qualify new sales opportunities and follow a sales process that mirrors how your customers want to buy, every sale should be frictionless.

Doesn't mean there won't be objections to overcome, hard questions to answer or negotiations over price and terms. Those aren't going anywhere.

But if you're meeting a market need, the right buyers for your business *want what you're selling*. They may even need it. It's critical to them achieving their own goals, objectives and/or success.

In that context, selling is never convincing. It's not pushy, high-pressure or aggressive. You communicate value, connect on benefits and let the buyer buy.

Four Tactics for Getting Started with Lead Nurture Marketing

Recently, Marketo offered a great overview and comparison of Nuture Marketing and Closed Loop Marketing. Both are strong and viable strategies for more effectively managing different types of B2B leads through a sales funnel through to close. And Marketo's right, nurture marketing is great, but closed loop marketing is better, and typically generates better results by more directly matching sales touch points and messages to specific prospect intent and behavior.

But achieving lead follow-up nirvana is a long ways from reality for many organizations. A survey earlier this year indicated that a mere 10% of companies were actively using lead nurture strategies as part of their demand generation and pipeline management marketing. Even for those 10% of companies, implementing a more complex closed loop system may feel intimidating and out of reach.

But for the other 90% of organizations, going from whatever they're currently doing (likely a variation of treating all leads equally) to executing a complex lead management strategy doesn't have to happen in one giant step. For these organizations, achieving a strong nurture marketing strategy (let alone the next step to closed loop) should be seen as a multi-step process. Below are a few recommendations to start migrating to a better way of triaging and working leads, which should result in more opportunities and more sales over time without changing lead generation tactics or budget.

1. **Define an ideal lead, and treat them differently :** Create a relatively simple definition of an ideal prospect, and start with two buckets – do they qualify or do they not? For example, does an ideal prospect need to come from a company of a particular size? From a particular titled contact? From a particular industry? Set just 2-3 criteria, and start triaging leads accordingly. Even this simple first step can ensure your sales team is working with the best leads more aggressively (and treating lower-priority leads as such).

2. **Start a single nurture campaign for all leads:** Sure, it would be great to have different nurture segments by industry, expected close date, reason the deal may be delayed, etc. But if you're just starting out nurturing leads, start with a single nurture campaign for all leads. A monthly newsletter, or a regular Webinar offer or even an occasional free white paper offer can keep you top of mind with prospects not yet ready to buy. Get complicated later, but get *something* going to those latent prospects right away.

3. **Establish qualification questions to segment leads into status buckets:** Are you talking to a decision-maker? Does budget exist? Is there an internal compelling event to make a decision soon? These are questions you can ask in a lead registration form, a follow-up survey or even in a call script your sales team uses. In any case, there are likely a handful of similar questions (no more than 4-5) that can be asked of prospects up front, recorded in your CRM system and be used to triage leads further. If nothing else, your sales team will love having this data to manage predictability of their short-term pipeline.

4. **Be honest about expected close dates, and set sales team follow-up expectations accordingly:** As new leads get contacted and qualified, get your sales team in the habit of establishing an expected close date. Your leads could fall into three buckets - immediate opportunities, medium-term opportunities and nebulous "future" opportunities. Understanding how quickly your prospect may make a decision can help determine the strength and frequency of your follow-up communication.

☑ Three Ways to Set Up a BIG Sales Month

In many selling environments, especially those with a relatively short sales cycle, the single most important thing *you have control of* to have a big sales month is what you do at the *beginning* of the month to set up above-quota sales through the rest of the month.

Here are three things you can do the beginning of every new month to hit your sales goals:

1. **Focus on Setting Appointments:** In the first couple days of the month, put a concerted focus on setting appointments with leads you already have. Use an external incentive or accelerator if need be, but work hard through your existing contact or lead list to create new appointments and presentations for the next few days. More appointments mean more active opportunities that can close by the end of the month.

2. **Incentives for Quickly Closing Slipped Deals:** Every new month starts with a handful of deals expected to close the previous month, but that for some reason slipped. Most sales organizations dump these into the overall "expected to close" bucket for the next month, but why shouldn't these deals close within the next few days? Put a focus on closing slipped deals immediately to give yourself a jump on your sales goal and to goose momentum for the month overall, for yourself and the rest of your team.

3. **More Leads Timed to Start of Month:** If you're marketing for a sales organization, do everything you can to generate new leads towards the start of the month (or quarter, depending on your typical selling cycles). At the beginning of the month, sales professionals are the most focused on building their pipelines. Leads that come in at the end of a month are more likely to get ignored as sales focuses on closing existing opportunities.

☑ Six Reasons Why Your Sales Suck

It's been a tough time for many reasons and on many levels, no doubt about it. Many companies – big and small, established and start-up – aren't exactly hitting their sales, revenue and customer growth targets. But it's a cop-out to blame the economy and a lack of customer demand. Many organizations, unfortunately, simply aren't executing on all cylinders when it comes to sales and marketing.

What's more, when economic conditions improve, those same problems and misfires that have existed will still be around, and can hurt your chances of accelerating sales and market share as the overall market and selling environment improves.

Below are six reasons your sales numbers might be suffering, each of which is within your control to address and improve – in good times and bad.

1. Are you selling to the right buyer?

Make sure you understand who the right decision-maker is for buying your product or service. Is that person different from the eventual end-user? Is there a third "influencer" of the purchase that needs to be on board before the buyer will sign?

How well you understand the purchase and decision-making ecosystem within the buying organization can make a big difference in whether or not you can quickly get to a "yes."

What's more, the right buyer in your target organization may have changed in the past year. In many cases, the individual who could make a purchase decision a year ago might need higher-level CFO approval today. If your sales process and messaging are focused on the HR Manager, for example, and the buyer today is actually the CFO, wouldn't that make a significant difference in how you sell?

2.   Are you selling benefits or features?

Look at your primary messaging, and think critically about whether it describes what you tactically do, or what your product/service enables as a benefit for the customer. There's a big difference – one focuses on how the product works, but the latter highlights why it's important.

Your customers may not actually care what you do, but they sure care about how it can help them achieve their own goals. Sell the benefits, not the features and tactics. Yes, prospects will eventually want to know how it works and how to use it. But you have to earn your way to that part of the conversation.

Get their attention first with benefits.

3.   Do you sound desperate?

It's very tempting right now to lower prices and create aggressive offers to move product. But those offers, though offering the potential for a quick bump in sales, have a downside as well. They can immediately put you in a position where you're competing on price, and failing to justify a premium price for a premium product (and result!).

Make too many offers and discounts too often in front of the same prospects, and you also lose the urgency to buy that those offers are meant to create in the first place. Yeah, there's a sale today, but the prospect will simply wait and see what the sale will look like tomorrow. End that pricing promotion this Friday, and if they expect it'll start again next week or next month, and they're more likely to sit on their hands.

4. Do your sales and marketing teams agree?

What is a good prospect? What is a good lead? What's the point at which a lead becomes a real sales opportunity?

If your sales and marketing organizations don't have a common definition and understanding of the answers to these questions, you definitely have a problem.

For marketing, providing quality leads to sales isn't the end. It should not be the objective. Quality leads is at the beginning of the sales process. Getting the best return and conversion on those leads requires that sales and marketing work closely together to support each other through the entire selling process – from awareness to interest, lead generation, trial and close.

5. Do your customers want what you're selling?

Let's assume that, when the product was introduced or created, there was a clear need for the solution or end-result it offered to your customer. Does that benefit still exist? Does the product or service still match the market need? Or has the market evolved?

The only way to answer this and related questions is to constantly listen to your customers and the market at large. Your product may have been critically important three years ago. But are there other solution alternatives today? Is your product still best at solving the problem? How do the answers to these questions change your product strategy, let alone your sales and marketing approach?

Not easy questions to ask or answer, but they get in the way of successful selling far more than you think, especially at a time when markets, technology and customer interests are evolving more rapidly than ever.

6.   **What are customers and prospects saying behind your back? And why aren't you participating?**

It used to be difficult and expensive to hear what your customers said about you – either to you directly or to each other. That, of course, has changed in a big way. Surprisingly, still few companies listen – let alone participate – in the conversation going on about their products, services and brands.

At minimum, make sure you know what your customers and prospects think about you. And what they think about your competitors. And probably more importantly, what they're saying about the problem you're trying to solve for them in the first place. How could understanding these three things help you better align product, marketing approach and messaging to address what your customers most care about?

Make sure you're looking at ways to directly participate in that conversation as well. If a customer or prospect is willing to share how you could make things better, why not use the same communication channel to thank them, show them what you've done differently and earn their trust, respect....and business?

 ## Four Requirements for Qualifying a Sales Opportunity

Your sales pipeline is only as good as it is qualified. If you have deals represented there that aren't real, and aren't moving, then you're just plain lying. You're lying to yourself that those deals will close, you're lying to your sales manager that your pipeline is healthy.

At any point in the month and quarter, an accurate assessment of pending sales is critically important. But unless there's a common definition for what a qualified sales opportunity is, this kind of assessment is next to impossible.

So what makes for a qualified sales opportunity? In a B2B setting, I believe you need at least four things:

1. **Engaged decision-maker:** This is someone in the organization who is qualified to make a purchase decision. They may need to get approval from a CFO, or have someone underneath them do an assessment, but you need the primary decision-maker engaged. Leads can come in from anywhere in the organization, but if that lead doesn't have decision-making power, then your deal isn't ready to move.

2. **Identified budget:** If you're replacing an incumbent product or service, this is a little easier. But if you're introducing a new expenditure, you'd better be sure there's money for it. Ask the hard question and get explicit confirmation that there are dollars to spend on what you're selling.

3. **Strong tie to organizational objectives:** This is the difference between "nice to have" and "need to have." There are many, many things that your prospects will think are cool, but will ultimately be priority #16 (which means they won't get funded, approved or implemented anytime soon). But if what you're offering ties to an existing, published objective (at least for the department, but ideally for the organization), then you have a chance. If what you have can help your decision-maker and organizational target achieve or exceed a publicly-stated goal, you're far more likely to get attention, get your project at the top of the list and get more people inside the organization rallying behind the purchase.

4. **Mutually agreed-upon purchase timeline:** Many sales professionals will put an "expected close date" next to prospective sales opportunities. But that close date is only real if the buyer would give the same timeline. To make a sales opportunity real, there needs to be a timeline in place. The buyer needs to be working concurrently with you on the same path. Just because you want a deal to close by the end of the month, or the end of the quarter, doesn't mean your buyer has the same urgency.

Every sales situation is a little different, so your qualified pipeline criteria may differ. But it's critically important that you at minimum create common expectations and definitions across your sales organization, so that the sales pipeline you're looking at (good or bad) is accurate.

NOTES

NOTES

~~~~~~~~~~~~~~~~~~~~~~~~~~~~~~~~~~~~~

Closing

~~~~~~~~~~~~~~~~~~~~~~~~~~~~~~~~~~~~~

Questions to Ask on the Last Selling Day of the Month

It's the last sales day of the month, which means staying focused on getting those last deals across the finish line. But with a new month and fresh start just ahead, here are several questions worth asking yourself (and your team) to ensure even greater focus, results and success ahead.

- Are you satisfied with your results this month?

- What was the most important factor in your success?

- If you could start the month again, what would you do differently?

- What one thing has kept you from having a better month?

- What will you do differently next month to ensure greater success?

- What tools do you need from others (managers, marketing, etc.) to be more successful?

- What specific, tactical commitments can you make today, and hold yourself accountable for each day next month, to be more successful?

- It's the last selling day of *next* month. Looking back, what will be the key factors that led to your success?

 ## Key to Closing Business? Focus on What You Can Control

You can't control your prospect's budget. You can't control their recent reorg. You can't control what your competitor is going to say, or do, or offer. You can't control the economy, or the weather, or your prospect's busy schedule.

But you can control how many prospects you talk to. You can control how well you address their specific needs and pain points in the presentation. You can control the timing, the frequency, the efficacy of your communication with prospects.

You can't control the timeline your buyers follow, but you can control the sense of urgency and scarcity communicated to that same prospect.

You can control your sales process, and how well you set expectations and committed next steps both for yourself and from your customers.

Whether you're in a marketing or a sales role, there's plenty you can't control. Don't fall into the trap of using those things as an excuse or crutch. Focus on what you can control, and manage those opportunities actively to get the results you want.

Stop Telling Prospects What You Do

Your prospects don't care what you do. They don't care how it works.

They're only thinking of themselves. And can you blame them? Their butt is on the line if they don't deliver results, cut costs, delight their own customers. They have their own problems, their own pain, their own priorities.

Your prospects don't care what you do. They will only care about you if you can solve their problem. Ease their pain. Make their job easier. Make them look like a hero.

Your prospects don't care what you do. They care *deeply* about what you can do for them.

There is only demand for your product is there's *more* demand for the solution it represents.

Sell that way.

☑ Five Tips for Better Customer-Centric Selling

When you're selling, your first challenge is always to connect with the prospect - build rapport and a basis for why they should care about you and what you have to offer. But too often, selling companies approach this conversation in a seller-centric way - fronting with what the company has to sell vs. what the customer needs.

Turning this around to focus more on customer-centric sales - especially at the front of the process - can be relatively easy. Below are five initial ways to pivot quickly to a customer-centric selling approach.

1. **Use "you" instead of "I":** Many sales people and marketers default their writing and speaking to the first-person, and focus their messages on what you (the seller) have and want. The next time you write a call script or sales letter, use "you" at least twice as often as you use "I". Make statements that address the customer and their situation and needs directly. It makes for a far more customer-centric approach that will attract and engage your readers more effectively.

2. **Treat the first sales call like an interview:** Even if you've already qualified the prospect, your first call should still be about them. Even if you only have a few minutes in person or on the phone, ask smart questions to not only better understand the prospect's situation, but also get them to directly admit the challenges and pain currently faced by life without your solution. In your first call, ask a handful of smart questions and spend at least 75% of the time listening. With the right questions, many prospects will walk right into the sale.

3. **Align yourself with existing customer priorities:** Too many sales professionals waste hours of time trying to sell something their prospects don't need. And even if they would benefit from it, you must align your solution with an existing problem or initiative in the organization. Your prospects are too busy to start juggling yet another priority not already on their plate. But by aligning your solution with something they're already trying to address and solve, you have a much better chance of being heard.

4. **Respect their time:** Assume your customers are at least as busy as you are. Just because they're interested in what you have doesn't mean they have an hour to hear you talk about it. Be brief, ask up front each time if they have a few minutes and think of ways to condense your information into less. Send less but more important collateral to review. Condense the hour-long Webinar to a 1-2 page executive summary. Find ways to get information to your prospects without taking up much time. They'll appreciate you for it.

5. **Let your current customers sell for you:** Case studies and success stories should be your most prominent and effective selling tool. Help your prospects envision what success with your product looks like a few days, weeks or months after they've bought it. Put those customer success stories in a variety of formats - print, audio, video, Web - and make it easy for prospects at various stages of the sales process to engage with them. Even if you're the best salesperson at the company, your customers have more credibility and will sell better than you. Get them in front of your prospects more often.

 ## Helping Your Customers Get Buying Approval

Most of the time when you're selling something, your buyer needs approval to move forward. If it's a big-enough consumer ticket item, that approval may need to come from a spouse, significant other or even a parent. In a B2B environment, it's often the buyer's boss.

So what are you doing to make it easier for your buyer's boss to say "yes"?

How are you arming your buyer with tools to help him sell the purchase upstream?

Salesforce.com, for example, has created an incredible set of ROI tools to help their customers justify a trip to the annual Dreamforce user conference each November. Their package comes complete with an already-drafted ROI letter for "buyers" to send directly to their bosses.

Could your customers use a similar ROI letter? What would that look like?

Might be worth thinking about...

Keeping Sales & Demand High during the Holiday Months

Customer needs don't disappear just because leaves are falling off trees and holidays are near. Below are several tips to keep your sales, customer demand and deal flow hopping in November and December.

- **Keep doing the same thing:** Treat November and December like any other month! Doing anything else is just a mentality. Your customers still need what you're selling, and those needs, demands and pains to solve haven't gone anywhere just because the holidays are near.

- **Appeal to end-of-year planning/budget cycles by your customers:** Many your prospects may have surplus budget to spend before the year is up. That, and/or they may be actively planning budgets for 2010. Either way, you want to be a part of that conversation if you have something they need.

- **Help them kick-start their own new year goals and results:** If what you're selling can benefit your customers and their own goals and objectives, isn't it better to have that in place on January 1 vs. waiting to buy and onboard later in the month, quarter or year? Build a sense of urgency that this is exactly the time to make a move and get a head start on next year's goals.

- **Know your customers; Make offers specific to what they're uniquely doing this time of the year:** If you know your customers well, you know what they're doing this time of year. If you sell to retail, this is clearly the most important time of the year. If you sell to summer vacation spots, this might be a time to actively plan and market for next year's busy season. Whatever your customers are doing and thinking about uniquely this time of year, customize your messages, offers and engagement tactics there.

- **Promote and execute webinars:** If you subscribe to the notion that your prospects don't feel like working hard this time of year, then they might be more likely to sign up for and attend a Webinar. If the office is a little slower on their end, they'll have more time to participate. It's a great time to educate and get them engaged with value-added content in a variety of formats (Webinar, blog, white papers, top 10 lists and more).

- **Help them reach their customers this time of year:** If you're worried about engaging prospects and customers this time of year, your prospects are probably worried about the same thing. Take what you know about them, their customers and their market/industry, and offer them advice on how to engage and sell to their end-customers as a means of engaging and building thought leadership. It's a great lead generation offer this time of year as well.

- **Holiday-Themed referral offers:** Engage current customers with seasonal offers to engage their peers and colleagues at other organizations on your behalf. Give them gift cards (to indulge themselves or to use in their own gift-buying) or any variety of offers that make sense for the nature, interest and geography of your customers.

- **Focus on demos:** So maybe your customers don't want to make a purchase decision until January. Even if that's true, you can focus November and December on getting your prospects as far down the purchase cycle as possible. Focus on doing as many demos as you can. Answer objections, get executive sponsors involved, send out proposals and begin negotiations on terms. Move prospects forward so that you're set up for a big beginning of Q1.

- **Front-Load Your Pipeline for Next Year's Fourth-Quarter:** Start planning (and budgeting) right now so that you're accelerating lead generation in Q3 of next year. That way, your pipeline is full of even more closeable business heading into Q4.

NOTES

NOTES

NOTES

~~~~~~~~~~~~~~~~~~~~~~~~~~~~~~~~~~~~~~~

Leveraging Social Media to Enhance Customer Service

~~~~~~~~~~~~~~~~~~~~~~~~~~~~~~~~~~~~~~~

Communication is Key

Social media has existed since the beginning of time. It's been around far longer than Twitter, Facebook, LinkedIn and the hundreds of other digital tools available to us today. If someone tells you social media is synonymous with the tools we may use currently to facilitate a conversation, walk away (nay, run away).

Social media, plain and simple, is merely the latest way we describe the means by which we communicate with each other. There's no question today's Web and mobile-based tools make communication faster, more transparent and interactive than ever before. But as consumers, we've expected (or at least desired) those kind of interactions with people, companies and brands for a long, long time. Only now, we're getting the real-time reaction and instant gratification we've always wanted.

As a customer service opportunity, the tools of social media can facilitate the acceleration, deepening and exponential pass-along of brand preference, loyalty and ROI for consumer and B2B businesses alike.

 ## The Benefits of Social Customer Service

- **Transparency:** Yes, the mere mention of transparency in some brands causes accelerated breathing and sweaty palms. But this is exactly what consumers and buyers want in their partners and brands. They don't expect you to be perfect, but they expect you to tell it like it is. Accept your weaknesses, admit to your faults, say you're sorry when you do something wrong. Do that in real-time (have the courage to do so!) and not only will your current customers be more loyal to you, but you'll be surprised how quickly transparency will convert the cautious and skeptical to your side.

- **Credibility:** By exposing yourself to the good, bad and ugly of the marketplace, you make everything else you do more sincere and credible. By enabling and embracing transparency, you by definition create credibility for yourself and your brand. Even those who still don't completely accept you, or prefer your competitors, can't help but admire your position and openness. And credibility (a close cousin of trust) is the foundation of any strong, long-term relationship.

- **Humanity:** Guess what? Behind every strong company, every brand, every building – are people. Real people build the product, provide the service and innovate what you see today into the products, services and solutions of tomorrow. Show the humanity of the people behind your brand through your social media outlets – directly in front of and in exchanges with your customers – and they'll be attracted to you all the more.

- **Community:** Perhaps the best part of social media's opportunity for customer service is that we're no longer talking at our customers. Every interaction is an opportunity to not only facilitate a two-way conversation, but open that conversation to other customers to foster and enhance the feeling of community. Combine transparency and humanity with community, and the bonds get stronger.

 ## How to Execute Social Customer Service

- **24-7 monitoring:** You have to watch, all the time. If something blows up on a Friday night, it's not OK to wait to respond until Monday morning. This mentality worked when communication was both interruptive and one-way, and when the call center shut down in the evening hours. But social media doesn't work that way. Your customers (and detractors) will talk whenever they feel like it. You (and your team and your fans) need to pay closer and wider attention to what's going on and what's being said so you can address, correct and/or amplify messages as appropriate.

- **Fast response time:** Even if you're just saying "let me check and I'll get back to you," respond quickly. Don't let open-ended questions and opinions hang out there without a response.

- **Customers helping customers:** You (and your team) don't need to be the only respondent when someone asks a question. Your customers can help each other as well. Give customers access to your social media channels, and encourage them to self-support each other with answers, best practices, usage tips and more.

- **Empower customers as community leaders:** If you know who your most active, supportive customers are, why not "promote" them to community leaders? Give them a discount or special consideration with your product, service or brand in exchange for actively participating in forums on your behalf. Customers helping customers will always work more credibly than brands helping customers, plus it takes more of the load off of your shoulders (particularly important for resource-constricted companies).

- **Throw a party for new customers:** Do your new customers feel welcome, or are they intimidated by their lack of experience and knowledge? Make them feel welcome in your social community. Invite them to introduce themselves, and share a story (or two) about what they're doing and how they're using what you're selling. This sharing alone will make them feel a part of the community, will immediately help you (and your community leaders) understand how they might be able to help and will increase their likelihood to come back to you first if they have questions, concerns or complaints.

- **Allow the community to save those who want to leave:** There will always be those who want to leave. For whatever their reason, they're ready to move to another product or service. Many companies have a "save team" of individuals focused on talking those customers into staying. But what if your loyal customers had that job? Wouldn't they more credibly be able to ascertain what the problem is, suggest alternative solutions and convert a higher percentage of those potential defectors back into the fold?

- **Publicize availability in all channels:** Do your customers know where your social communities are? Do they know how to find you at 1:00 in the morning? How are you helping brand new customers discover these channels and resources? The more customers discover and engage these social customer service opportunities, the more likely they'll engage with the community and accelerate their satisfaction and loyalty (not to mention decrease cost of your more traditional, resource-intensive customer service options).

- **It's not just about Twitter!** Know your customers, and know which social channels they're more likely to engage with. Twitter is valuable, sure, but so is Facebook, LinkedIn, discussion forums, wikis, blogs and more. Find out where your customers are more likely to engage, and put your focus there (at least initially).

 ## Organizational Implementation Advice

- **Customer service is the new marketing:** Let's face it, if you successfully implement social customer service, your customer service organization will be engaged with your customer more often and more frequently than traditional marketing channels. Doesn't that mean customer service is now as, if not more, important to shaping customer perceptions, brand preference and purchase activity? If you started your organization from scratch, I bet customer service and marketing would be the same thing, and in the same department. Treat it that way now and things work better, more smoothly and more successfully.

- **Keep legal out of it:** Tell them what you're doing, but keep them out of the day-to-day. Don't let them edit your Facebook account, your Tweets or your back-and-forth. They don't review every conversation and email from your customer service organization today, so why would social media channels be any different?

- **Executive support is key:** They don't need to be involved every day (although their active presence in your social channels can accelerate credibility and humanity), but your executive team needs to strongly and publicly endorse what you're doing. Many others are likely to want to slow down or limit how transparent and pervasive social channels are executed in your customer service plan. Active executive sponsorship can nip that in the bud, quickly.

- **Choose and train participants:** Don't assume everyone in your customer service organization will know how to best engage customers in these open channels. Don't go overboard with rules and brand restrictions, but give participants some training, guidelines and even some role-playing to show what's expected and what's possible.

- **Reward engagement and behavior:** This applies both to your internal staff as well as your loyal customers. Encourage, recognize and reward positive interactions, speedy responses to issues, and success stories where your newly-leveraged social customer service channels have won over a skeptic, saved a fading customer, or created a new brand loyalist for life.

- **Pave your own path:** These are guidelines, but there's no playbook. There are no rules. As you execute, you'll discover what works and doesn't work for your company and brand.

NOTES

NOTES

~~~~~~

Renewals & Loyalty

~~~~~~

Customer Loyalty is more Than Just a Number

The means by which most of us measure customer loyalty is a bit flawed. Retention is up, attrition is down and we think all is well.

With sales, it's easier to boil performance and success down to a number. Either you closed the sale, or you didn't. New revenue is booked and realized, or it's not.

With retention, it's a little fuzzier, because not every customer is alike. Yes, you may have retained 95% of customers last month. But how many of those customers are raving fans? How many are frustrated and just sitting out the rest of their contract?

Those are *very different* customers. One is willing to sing your praises to other current and prospective customers – helping sales and solidifying retention (and possibly success) with some of your other customers.

The less-satisfied customer, unfortunately, may be doing the opposite. Their frustration is simmering, and they're telling others about it. They're sharing with their colleagues, with peers and other customers via their social channels, and literally closing the door on future revenue opportunities – possibly without you knowing about it.

Our spreadsheets tell us these two customers are the same. But they clearly are not.

How are you identifying these two customers in your business? And how are you using that insight to address and improve both the less-satisfied customers, as well as the potential weak points in the product or service itself?

How Customer Loyalty is Your Ultimate Competitive Advantage

It's not a secret that loyal customers are good for an organization or brand. You don't see too many executives saying they don't want more of them. But what's interesting to me is how few companies truly acknowledge, take care of and leverage those loyal customers in a way that measurably accelerates market share and recurring revenue while mitigating competitive risk and reducing sales and marketing costs.

New customer sales and marketing? At most companies that means a meaningful lead generation budget, a full sales team, lots of support and attention.

Existing customers? A newsletter, maybe some training and an 800-number if they have questions.

This is a broad generalization, but you get the point (and you've seen it, both at companies you work with and for, as well as directly as a customer of others).

There's no question in my mind that every business has significant and measurable revenue potential with greater focus in this area.

How?

- **Treat them right** – deliver a fantastic product or service – and you can count on their business for life.

- **Be remarkable,** and they'll tell their friends and colleagues about you as well.

- **Earn their trust,** and they'll tell you exactly what they're seeing in the market – your competitors, new innovations, etc.

- **Engage them regularly,** and they'll tell you when you're wrong, when you screw up and give you time to fix it.

- **Actively listen,** react to their feedback, innovate when they ask and they won't go anywhere.

- **Create an army of ambassadors,** and they're an extension of your sales force in situations that you have zero access to today.

- **Make them your eyes and ears,** and they'll give you the earliest heads-up possible to any competitive threat on the horizon (with enough time to react, adjust and cut competitors off at the knees before they can get momentum).

- **Ask them to brainstorm with you,** and they'll give you far better, more creative ideas than you'd ever come up with yourself.

- **Surprise them with your responsiveness, speed and approachability,** and they'll treat you like a loyal friend.

You can do this. You can do all of this, and most of it doesn't cost any more than a change in how you manage your customers. How you talk to them. How often, with a different message, a different tone and both more frequency and thoughtfulness.

Your customers desperately want this from you. They've made a commitment to you (in a big or small way), and all they ask is that you return that commitment to them.

 ## Eight Mistakes to Avoid with Your Customer Loyalty Program

Let's say you're building a loyalty incentives program for your product. Everybody has great ideas about what will motivate the desired customer behavior, outcome and lifetime value.

You're clearly not the first company to build such a program. What if you could read through a bunch of post-launch, post-mortem reports from those experiences? What if you could understand which components of your current plan should be scrapped, reversed or modified before they see the light of day?

I unfortunately do not have this magical stack of reports, but I do hear many of the same things over and over as marketers move to "V2" of their loyalty programs. Here are eight statements I hear most often.

1. **"We should have focused on the customer's priorities, not just our own."** This may seem like a straightforward concept, but it's not how most loyalty programs are built. Loyalty programs, by their nature, are intended to drive activity that has been pre-determined to drive value for the company. Shop here more often, increase your order size, refer your friends so we don't have to spend more marketing dollars. All great ideas. Problem is, many loyalty programs are built such that they so directly and transparently focus on these end-goals of the company, that there's little value or actual incentive built in for the customer.

   Building your loyalty strategy needs to be a two-step process. First, by all means determine your objectives. Know the business outcome you expect to create. But then, translate that into something customer-centric. Find the ties between your business objectives and your customers' priorities. Those direct ties - where there's little to no friction between what both parties want - is likely the foundation of how your loyalty program will grow and thrive.

2.   **"We made it too complicated."** Collect points, bundle them together, mail them in, then win a prize. Thanks for playing. Refer us to your colleagues, answer three trivia questions, then come back next week and answer three more. Then you're entered in our drawing.

OK, not every loyalty program is that complicated. But think about the programs you like the best. They don't require a lot of work. They don't require math. You do what you've been doing, and things happen. Buy an airline ticket, and you get miles. Buy enough tickets, and you get a free flight. Shop at my grocery store all the time, and you get lower prices on certain items.

Problems with loyalty program complications arise when a) you make the customer think too much, b) you add too many steps to collect the motivation or c) you require either math or memory. Don't do these things. Make it simple, at least at first.

3.   **"When we stopped marketing, the program stopped working."** If you have to keep asking your customers to participate, then your loyalty program a) isn't really resonating, and b) isn't sustainable. If it doesn't eventually create a habit - where customers know it exists, want it and naturally take the right steps to get it on their own - then it's either too complicated or not tied to an important-enough customer interest.

When you launch a new loyalty program, of course it's going to need its own stand-alone marketing campaign to build awareness and participation. But eventually, ongoing marketing of the program to existing customers should happen less frequently, less interruptively and largely via existing communication channels.

If as you build your new loyalty program, this end-goal doesn't feel achievable, keep thinking.

4.   **"We didn't need to spend as much money to get the same behavior."** Your customers are money-driven, all of them. They want more of it, they want to spend less of it, they want products and services that will help them get and save more of it. They also don't

mind free stuff, so if you want to drive behavior, you can a) give them money, b) save them money or c) give them something cool for free.

Or, you could put a star next to their name on your Web site. You could make their membership card a different color. You could let them into the store an hour early. You could give them a special phone number that puts them at the front of the call queue.

Your customers are motivated by money, but not just money. They also want to feel special, have special privileges, so demonstrate they're different or better than their peers or colleagues. The better you understand your customer and what ultimately motivates them, the more things beyond money you'll realize can be powerful drivers of behavior. And many of those cost next to nothing.

5. **"Our best customers just wanted to be recognized."** This is a subset of comments above, but an important one. Recognition, differentiation and ego are powerful motivators. They work with business and consumer audiences alike. They are likely motivating behavior with your product independent of any existing or non-existing loyalty program.

    And recognition can come cheap. A club that's little more than a name. A personal letter from the CEO or store manager. A hand-written thank you card. Their name written on the wall. Cheap but effective.

6. **"It was too much work."** Ambitious new programs often require new tools, extra bandwidth and more people thinking about and acting upon the program to make it work. If this work is required of existing people, existing systems and existing budgets without adding additional time or resources to execute, you're doomed to failure (or at least frustration from the get-go).

    As you've already seen from examples listed above, great loyalty programs don't need to be complicated. They don't need to require significant new infrastructure, policies or procedures to make them work. And if they do need new resources, the program had better be important enough and cross-functionally supported well enough to get the support it needs to succeed.

7. **"We should have tested it before the full roll-out."** Even if you follow the advice above and more, you'll still not get it right. You'll still find ways to improve. Better to know that with a subset of customers before those mistakes are made with your entire base.

    Pick a handful of customers for a test group. Not your most vocal, not your most favorite. Try to find a cross-section, or a segment that's naturally unbiased (i.e. a particular store, or all customers in a particular city or state). Don't just tell them about the program, but try and actually roll it out. The feedback you get in a focus group or survey will be different from what they tell you when they're faced with what you're actually requiring them to do.

8. **"We didn't involve others throughout the organization."** It's fine if the marketing team plans and spearheads the launch of your loyalty program. But execution should be a cross-functional effort. Every customer-facing team and individual should know about it and help you promote it. Teams and individuals beyond marketing could themselves have incentives for how well they get customers involved.

    Marketing today can't be contained to the marketing team. Every member of your organization is helping to market your product, service, brand and company. The customer-facing teams do it directly. But your developers build product that impacts how your customers feel about you. Your finance team makes decisions that impact how well you can support them.

    Each one of these groups will play a role in making your loyalty program successful. And if it truly drives the right behavior and business results, they'll be proud and motivated to continue their support and participation.

☑ How to Turn Customers into Ambassadors for Your Business

Guess what? You already know how, because you're already doing it.

More specifically, your best customers are already doing it. You may not know it, you may not know exactly who's doing it and you may not know how they're doing it or how they got that way. But it's happening.

Some of your customers went from prospects, to new customers, to happy customers, to ambassadors. Your job is to find out how, and why, and establish that path for more customers moving forward.

In other words, don't artificially engineer a path to make customers happy. Don't create an incentive program or a loyalty program or other customer success initiatives out of the air. Find out what's occurring naturally, what's already driving higher loyalty and ambassadorship among your customers and build processes to make it happen more often.

The first step is to segment your ambassadors from your "average" customer.

Then ask the following questions:

- What was their path to becoming a brand ambassador? How did they get there?

- Who's on that path today, and where did it start? What were the important milestones?

- Are there shortcuts or catalysts on that path? Are there experiences, results, features or otherwise that accelerate the path to advocates?

- Who helped those customers along the way? Who were their mentors and/or guides? Who (besides you, besides your company) can help show them the way?

- What are those ambassadors doing to share their passion with others? With either other customers or prospective customers?

Many of these questions you can answer by looking at past behavior and performance. Dig into your customer database and analytics, and find out what your ambassadors have in common.

You will find ambassadorship accelerants that will surprise you. That are easy to replicate. That cost next to nothing.

This analysis can take some time, but it's worth it. In the meantime, do the following:

- Under promise and over deliver.

- Respond. Quickly. Personally.

- Be accessible.

- Be human.

- Make things simpler.

- Focus on results.

These things always work. And notice most of them are about service, not product. Even in a product-oriented business, service can mean everything. And much of what will work is faster, easier and cheaper to make happen than you may realize.

 ## How & When to Thank Your Customers

We all know the season to send your customers a "we're thankful for your business" email. We get them at the same time each year. Clients even ask me if these are a good idea for their customer base as well. I tell them they certainly are, but here's the rub.

Of course you're thankful for your customers' business, and reminding them of such during the holidays in particular is a great idea. But you're equally thankful for their business the rest of the year! Your customers need to be reminded of that (with your words *and* your deeds) on a regular basis. That's the best way to demonstrate your true thankfulness and appreciation.

Take the opportunity today to send a thank you email, blog post, tweet, whatever. Make it your season.

NOTES

NOTES

NOTES

Sales Management

☑ Six Levels of Managing Sales Performance

There are as many ways to manage sales performance as there are sales managers. But it still comes down to results.

If you're focused on managing a sales rep's performance and output, you start at the top and work your way down until you've found something to optimize. The cascade could look something like this:

1. Closed business (vs. quota or goal)

2. Pipeline (closeable business within current month/quarter/year)

3. Pipeline make-up (big deals, small deals, the right deals?)

4. Pipeline activity (next steps, demos, proposals)

5. Leads (how many, quality, which are next to become an Opportunity)

6. Activities (cold calling, new meetings, lead follow-up)

Individual sales rep review sessions can follow an agenda like this, with a focus on enabling/helping the rep to overcome obstacles and solve problems to exceed her goal.

The focus is ALWAYS on the top of this list. At the end of the day, it's all about closed business. But the elements below closed business are what get you there, and is usually where the roadblocks occur that lead to missing milestones.

What do you think? Are there critical steps missing? What's your preferred method of managing sales reps to maximum performance and closed business output?

☑ Four Best Practices for Running Successful Sales Meetings

Jonathan Farrington published an excellent set of best practices for running sales meetings. Below are four of his best suggestions:

1. **Make sure that at least fifty per cent of the meeting is taken up with some kind of sales training.** You can deliver this yourself or you might consider using specialists from outside of the company.

2. **Insist on punctuality,** for there is nothing which detracts from a meeting so much as people coming in late with lame excuses or returning late from a coffee break. Not only is this disruptive for the meeting, but it is bad for group discipline as well and each time a manager allows this, he relinquishes a little leadership capacity. Start the meeting on time to the minute. Do not wait for late arrivals and whatever you do, do not be late yourself.

3. **Begin the meeting in the way you plan to carry on throughout** - with a friendly smile and a dynamic greeting, do not commence in a flat uninspired monotone. Be informal, relax and encourage team members to do likewise. Do remember that a sales meeting is one of those few occasions where you can provide "collective motivation" so you need to be at your inspiring best.

4. **Do not do all the talking yourself.** Salespeople (and most other people) hate to be lectured at. Ask questions and listen to the answers. Ask for opinions, and always question the reason for a particular opinion. Do remember generally people comprehend:

    *   11% of what they hear.
    *   32% of what they see.
    *   73% of what they see and hear.
    *   90% of what they see, hear and discuss.

Management & Leadership

They're two different things, aren't they?

Management can be quite tactical. It can be primarily about execution, and about managing *things*.

But leadership is about having vision. It transcends managing things, and becomes about managing *people*. Not just managing, but motivating and *inspiring* people. That's leadership.

Too often, we think about management and leadership as the same thing. But they're quite different. Great managers aren't always great leaders. Great leaders aren't always great managers.

Businesses need both.

Which are you? Are you one or the other? Are you both? Are you either?

 Hiring the Right People

Hiring the right people in your business is possibly the single most important factor in achieving success. Yes, external and other factors (some outside of your control) play a huge part too. But the right people can take those factors and make the necessary adjustments to help your business grow and thrive.

This point seems to have more consensus than the method by which you filter and evaluate those prospective hires. The book *Topgrading*, for example, recommends lengthy interviews to get at the heart of a candidate's true potential.

But Chip and Dan of *Made to Stick* fame argued the exact opposite point - that interviews are largely worthless (at least in terms of predicting future performance), and that work samples, job-knowledge tests and peer ratings of past job performance are far more valuable.

I don't think there's a right answer leaning exclusively on either side of the argument, but focusing on work samples and the like *first* will likely serve as a time-saving filter on candidates that clearly don't make the grade, and weren't worth your time to interview to begin with.

Focus your time on the remainder, and you're far more likely to be speaking primarily with candidates who can make a difference.

 ## Nine Critical Hiring Strategies for Every Employee in Your Organization

Few hiring managers consider the significant costs of making a bad hiring decision. And in today's market, success in hiring may be the single most important lever you have to making your business more successful.

Sure, our economy might be in a tough spot right now, but thousands of companies are still hiring in nearly every market and vertical industry. Those companies (and you'll be one of them either now or soon) are facing a record number of applicants for a finite number of positions.

Unfortunately, this makes hiring the right people even harder and more critical to the health and success of your business this year. Yes, there are more applicants to choose from, but you can ill afford to make a bad hiring decision right now. Choose the wrong person for the job, and you're at minimum wasting the organization's time training that individual and managing them through mediocre results.

Worst yet, that mediocre hire is likely affecting the productivity and success of others around them. Ultimately, there's the cost of replacing that role and going through the entire hire and train cycle all over again.

Growing your business is hard enough, don't let a bad hire make it even harder. Here are nine recommendations for making every hire this year and beyond a superstar for your organization well into the future.

1. **Spend time interviewing:** Most interview cycles give hiring managers and other interviewers 30-60 minutes to determine whether an applicant is right for the position. Is that really enough time to get to know whether someone can truly help your business? Is that enough time to determine whether their resume is puffery, or if they truly have the innate ability to excel at your company?

I know you're busy, and there's never a great time to take a break from "productive" work to interview a prospective employee. But failing to take the time today can cost you countless hours and days of frustration down the road.

Spend a minimum of two hours with a candidate before making a hiring decision. Bradford D. Smart, author of the book Topgrading, would say that's still not enough - that you should spend at least four hours getting to know prospective employees. Even if you do this with 3-4 well-chosen candidates, think about the impact that right person can have on your business, your own productivity and success down the road. Aren't a few extra hours today worth that investment?

2. **Ask for work product:** Don't just ask to see past work done, ask candidates to provide you with something new. Give them an assignment or challenge you're currently grappling with, and ask them to come back to you with some great ideas and suggestions.

    This isn't about getting them to work for free. You're not asking for a 20-page presentation on your new product launch. You're simply asking for a demonstration of how smart, creative and productive this prospective new employee could be, with something that's far more relevant to your own business than what is currently in his resume.

    Hungry candidates, especially in this market, will do this for you. Those who won't do it probably aren't right for your business anyway.

3. **Demonstrate creativity:** Every employee, at every level of your organization, will need to demonstrate creativity to be successful. Few projects go as planned, and even the most menial of tasks often require employees to make countless decisions on their own, every day.

    Will your new employee have the chops to make those decisions on her own? And will she more often than not make the right decision for your business?

    Think about interview questions that can demonstrate how creative each candidate is, relative to the role they will soon have. This can be related to the "work product" described above, or can be a handful of case study questions that help you literally watch how the candidate thinks.

Don't worry if they get answers wrong, at least based on how you currently think about the business. Determining their creativity and problem-solving at this stage is more about how they think, rather than necessarily where they end up. Training and more intelligence about your unique business will improve their critical thinking skills. But you want an ideal candidate to be creative at her core.

4. **How badly do they want it?** You want an employee who's hungry. Not just hungry for a paycheck, but hungry to help your organization grow. Throughout the hiring process, how do your candidates demonstrate that hunger? Are they following up before and after the interview? What's the content of that follow-up? Is it me-centric ("please give me this job") or you-centric (reiterations of how they can help you succeed - new ideas, follow-ups on interview conversations, etc.).

    There is, of course, a line between tenacity and annoyance. Someone who's following up too often might be high maintenance on the job. But equally, a candidate who doesn't follow up likely won't have the tenacity and initiative on the job that you need.

5. **Grace and inspiration under pressure:** Resumes have been carefully crafted well in advance. Work samples carefully chosen, references vetted and prepared. Good job candidates work hard to put their best foot forward before they walk in your door, and the level to which they've prepared can itself tell you a lot about each candidate (good and bad).

    But how that prospective hire reacts to impromptu questions and challenges gives you an altogether different and important perspective. Most interviews feature the same questions - tell me about your past, talk about a challenging situation you worked through, where do you want to be in five years, etc. Often times, even bad candidates will anticipate these questions and have great answers prepared.

    But make sure you get a sense for how those candidates think on their feet, and how they react to pressure situations that put them on the spot. How they react - independent of how they answer the direct question - will give you an important glimpse into how they might react to real-time situations every day in your organization.

    One of my favorite interview tactics is to ask a candidate if I can get them a drink, then leave them with a real-time challenge question as I walk away. I come back after 3-4 minutes and ask for the answer. The challenge should be unique to your organization (think "work product" if you want), but will demonstrate how the candidate thinks, and acts, under pressure.

6.   **Look behind the references:** Every candidate has a handful of people from their past teed up to provide strong recommendations from their past work. You can pretty much guarantee you'll hear the same thing from those they've listed or provided you. But even in that list, you can learn something the candidate may or may not have meant to imply.

Who are their references? What stage of the candidate's career are they from - their most recent job or a job 15 years ago? What level are the references - peers, mentors, managers, partners or customers?

I recently came across a resume for a salesperson where four of the five listed references were his past customers at a past job. His success is based on delighting customers, and his past customers were there with endorsements to prove it.

When looking at references provided, look for and explore the holes as well. If their immediately-past job isn't reflected as a reference, and their search isn't confidential, that's a path worth following.

7.   **Check the online footprint:** Smart hiring managers use resumes for largely getting a sense for a candidate's professional history, but using their online footprint to get a sense for the individual and personality they may be bringing into the workplace.

This starts with a Google search, but should extend to some of the other "usual suspects" where candidates typically lay their true personalities bare - Facebook, Flickr, Twitter and more.

What do you find there? Any skeletons or red flags? Any signs that the individual may not live up to your company's values? This gets to the issue of a candidate's character, and it's important. There's no way character and personality separates itself from an individual when they walk into the office door. You need to know who you're hiring beyond the resume.

8. **Focus on the future, not the past:** When it comes to a candidate's professional experience and success, the best it can do is give a hint to what's possible from the individual within your business. It's critical that you translate that past experience to expected future performance by ensuring, during the interview and evaluation process, that the candidate can still speak to and exhibit the skills, insights, creativity and drive that made him successful previously.

   Too many professionals, for whatever reason, lose their focus and drive at some point in their career. Past success, for them, doesn't always predict future performance. By asking candidates about their real-time ideas, what they'll do for you, how they would approach a new situation or challenge, you get a sense for how they think and act now, not back then.

   And by doing this in the contexts described above (longer interviews, asking for work product, etc.), you'll have a better sense up-front for whether the candidate can truly live up to what he's accomplished in the past.

9. **Make sure compensation is correct:** It's a buyer's market for new hires right now, but that doesn't mean you can get sloppy with the compensation package. Today's compensation trends are more dynamic than ever. In many industries and for many common roles, compensation growth trends have slowed. For other industries, however, compensation has actually accelerated.

   Best to know for sure which is which for your new positions (and all positions in your organization for that matter). Use compensation data, surveys and tools to help you ensure the price you offer is the right price, possibly saving you on labor costs this year and beyond.

 ## Capturing Daily Feedback from Your Team & Industry

A recent newsletter from Verne Harnish suggested ideas for capturing daily feedback from your sales team, customers, prospects and the market in general, all at the same time. Nik VanHaeron, president of Canadian-based Uvalux Tanning and Support, shared this:

"I thought I'd share with you one of my favorite management tools. I call it our Highs, Lows and Need to Knows. These are my "tea leaves"... I see a lot of trends, allows me to celebrate successes, find out what's bogging our sales department, and what they are hearing in the industry.

"Everyday, I send a simple survey to our sales team. It has three simple questions on it. What was your high point of the day? What was your low point? And anything you heard that management should need to know? It arrives in their inbox at 4:55pm every day, so the last thing they do before they go home is reflect on their day and get things off their mind. I use Constant Contact to send the survey. It's the first thing that I read in the morning, and I love it. It gives me any key items that I have to look at first thing in the morning. We discuss it at our huddle, and get it done! It's about seeing trends sooner than your competition and the market."

 ## Three Great Interview Strategies

Warren Ethridge from *The Warren Report* has some fantastic insight focused on helping us get the most out of interviews. No matter *why* you're interviewing someone, this is great advice:

1. **Shock them and get their attention**: Let them know right away that this isn't going to be a typical interview. Get them out of their comfort zone, for both of your sakes. If they weren't giving you their full attention, they will now - for the entire remainder of the interview.

2. **Win their trust**: Know something about them going in; study them (at least a little) to know why they're there and what they can contribute (for their and your specific interests). The more they trust you earlier in the interview, the more earnest and interesting they'll be throughout.

3. **Earn their respect**: Prove that you care, and want to learn more about them. Listen to their answers. Better yet, don't come in with a written or prepared set of questions. Spend your time listening and reacting, and let your instincts and their answers take you to the next question. You'll both get more out of it.

How to Teach & Reinforce Consistent Messaging with Your Sales Team

It's one thing to get your company's customer and benefit-centric messaging right in an email, blog post or other marketing campaign. But how do you take those same messages and successfully get an entire sales team to speak from the same playbook?

Scripting isn't the answer (more on that below). You need every sales rep to understand, believe in and use the messaging that will best resonate with your customers, generate higher response and move more business forward.

Below are several recommendations for marketing and sales managers to get every sales professional on your team using the same language.

- **Role playing:** When you first introduce new messaging, don't train it by handing out a bullet list and talking through it. Get your reps comfortable with the messaging by acting it out in simulated prospect conversations. Some organizations go as far as to have a live role-playing "test" for new reps to make sure they're comfortable using new messaging. But even if you don't go that far, use role-playing to introduce messaging and then incorporate "refresh" sessions on occasion to keep it fresh and top of mind.

- **Don't over script it:** Good sales reps aren't going to use a word-for-word script anyway. It's OK to give them messaging in a training environment that is written out - in bullet or paragraph form - but you can't expect them to use this verbatim in a sales pitch. It will come across to the prospect as wooden, contrived and/or inauthentic. Instead, highlight in your messaging the key words and phrases that are most important, and use the role-playing to reinforce that these words and phrases are making their way into conversations.

- **Sell it with research and examples:** Want your sales team to believe in the new messages? Prove to them that it's real and will work with their prospects by backing it up with research and outside examples. Give them confidence that these messages will resonate with their prospects and help them sell more.

- **Try a conversation tree approach:** When you structure new messaging for presentation to the sales team, consider putting it into a "conversation tree" format. In other words, map out the progression of questions or back-and-forth you expect will happen on the call. This will show reps not only what messages you want used, but how to contextually introduce them into a natural conversation.

- **Keyword reminders at each desk:** Even if you use bullet or paragraph-formatted messaging to educate and train the sales team, don't expect this same format will be useful when they're on a live call and need a reminder. Instead, give them something they can pin up at their desk that focuses on the keywords. If trained well, these keywords will remind them "on the fly" of the broader messages, phrases and themes they need to use on the phone.

- **Monitoring and reinforcement:** If you have the ability to do remote call monitoring, use these sessions to check for correct and consistent usage of the new messaging. Afterward, call out those who are using it well and anonymously cite examples where it may not have been used, with suggestions for how it could have been incorporated. This will reward those who are using the new messaging with some peer recognition, while providing an ongoing training opportunity without calling out those who may still be struggling.

NOTES

NOTES

~~~~~~

Credits & Copyrights

~~~~~~

You can find more information on much of the contents of this book, as well as additional information and insights, at www.mattonmarketingblog.com.

We hope this book inspires you to keep thinking, innovating, and inspiring those around you. The author was particularly inspired by Neil Rackman, Ardath Albee, Verne Harnish, David Allen, Andy Sernovitz, Mike Andrews, Jill Konrath, Jeff Thull, Robert Pease, Michael Gerber, Jackie Huba, David Rosenberg and many many others.

Special thanks to TinyTee Graphics/Teena Brugh for her fantastic cover art and layout work, and to Jillian Blodgett for her editing.

About the Author

Matt Heinz

Matt brings more than 12 years of marketing, business development and sales experience from a variety of organizations, vertical industries and company sizes. His career has focused on delivering measurable results for his employers and clients in the way of greater sales, revenue growth, product success and customer loyalty.

Matt has held various positions at companies such as Microsoft, Weber Shandwick, Boeing, The Seattle Mariners, Market Leader and Verdiem. In 2007, Matt began Heinz Marketing to help clients focus their business on market and customer opportunities, then execute a plan to accelerate sales, revenue and customer growth.

Matt lives in Kirkland, Washington with his wife Beth, daughter Clara, and a menagerie of animals (including a dog, two cats, and three chickens).

Further your Marketing Knowledge

Matt's Blog
http://www.mattonmarketingblog.com

Monthly Sales & Marketing Newsletter
http://www.heinzmarketinginsights.com

LinkedIn Profile
http://www.linkedin.com/in/mattheinz

Matt's Business
http://www.heinzmarketing.com

Matt on Twitter
http://www.twitter.com/heinzmarketing

NOTES

NOTES

NOTES

NOTES

NOTES